mass communication

A Sociological Perspective
second edition

Charles R. Wright
University of Pennsylvania

Random House
New York

Second Edition
987654
Copyright © 1959, 1975 by Random House, Inc.

All rights reserved under International and Pan-American Copyright
Conventions. No part of this book may be reproduced in any form
or by any means, electronic or mechanical, including photocopying,
without permission in writing from the publisher. All inquiries should
be addressed to Random House Inc., 201 East 50th Street, New York,
N.Y. 10022. Published in the United States by Random House, Inc.,
and simultaneously in Canada by Random House of Canada Limited,
Toronto.

Library of Congress Cataloging in Publication Data

Wright, Charles Robert, 1927–
  Mass communication.
  Bibliography: p.
  Includes index.
  1. Mass media—Social aspects. I. Title.
HM258.W74   1975   301.16   74-34386
ISBN 0-394-31883-8

Cover by Jeheber & Peace

Manufactured in the United States of America. Composed by Cherry
Hill Composition, Pennsauken, N.J. Printed and bound by the Colonial
Press, Clinton, Mass.

To ANNE MARIE

preface

The study of mass communications has flourished and expanded during the decade and a half since the first edition of this book appeared. The sociology of mass communication has matured in the process. But development need not mean discontinuity. Many of the salient and persistent questions of the 1950s and 1960s remain unsolved today; they merit consideration in the light of new research. And the recent contributions of sociologically oriented researchers have been built upon past foundations—by testing and modifying earlier propositions and offering new perspectives.

Although the sociology of mass communication is a relatively new specialty, its findings are too varied and complex to be condensed into a short book. We are therefore compelled to be selective. This edition, like the first, is intended as an introduction to the field.

The new edition is more than an updating of descriptive accounts and research findings. It includes one completely new chapter on the sociology of the communicator; each remaining chapter has been thoroughly rewritten, incorporating new research, occasionally adding new sections and deleting some others. We have not hesitated, however, to keep an old (sometimes classic) example if it best serves to illustrate a sociological point. The guiding criterion for selectivity has been sociological relevance, not in terms of the disciplinary identity of the researcher but in terms of the theoretical orientation and implications of the research itself. Thus this work complements works on mass communication that stress a psychological, economic, humanistic, journalistic, or other orientation to the topic. If our sociological perspective has a theme, it is the need to examine mass communications within the broader framework of social structure and cultural context.

The book begins with a challenge: after exploring the characteristics that distinguish mass communications from other forms of human communication, it invites the reader to apply one sociological orientation—functional analysis—to the examination of the social effects of mass communication. Chapter 2 considers mass communications as social institutions and provides an overview of several foreign communications systems against which our own can be compared. Chapter 3 examines the sociology of the mass communicator from the perspectives of the sociology of occupations and professions, the analysis of complex organizations, and the sociology of work. Chapter 4, on the sociology of the audience, stresses sociological research on the links between interpersonal communications and mass communications behavior, including the role of both in the diffusion of news, innovations, and opinions and in affecting opinions and behavior. Chapter 5 supplies examples of qualitative and quantitative analyses of mass media content especially bearing on sociologically relevant aspects of popular culture. It focuses first on studies of the kinds of characters presented as heroes and villains by our mass media. Then it examines data on the portrayals of various occupational and minority groups and, finally, on the treatment of goals and means, drawing implications for the sociological study of anomie. Chapter 6 returns to the topic introduced in Chapter 1—the social effects of mass communication. Here speculation is tempered with empirical research findings. Not all social effects are considered, of course; but those discussed provide an introduction to the rich and complex problems for sociological theory and research that are posed by this topic.

This new edition has a greatly increased number of footnote references to the literature. These, together with the list of selected readings, should aid the reader who wishes more information about any of the topics covered or about such other aspects of mass communication study as research methods, international communication, public opinion, and policy.

It is my pleasure publicly to acknowledge an indebtedness of long standing to several friends and colleagues. I have benefited from thoughtful and critical readings of the revised manuscript (or the earlier edition) by Herbert H. Hyman, Mary E. W. Goss, Charles H. Page, and Raymond J. Murphy. The revised edition was aided by the research assistance of several former students, especially Judith Beinstein, Josephine Holz, March Kessler, and Linda Park. A direct and immeasurably important intellectual source for my sociological perspective on mass communications is the training and research experience I have enjoyed under

three masters of the subject: Herbert H. Hyman, Paul F. Lazarsfeld, and Robert K. Merton. In recent years I have profited
greatly from exchanges with my colleagues at the University of
Pennsylvania's Annenberg School of Communications.

None of the generous people mentioned above, of course, is
in any way responsible for whatever defects the book may have.

C. R. W.

July 1974

contents

mass
communication

1

the nature and functions of mass communication

Communication is a social process that is fundamental and vital to human survival. It is fundamental insofar as every human society—primitive or modern—is founded on the capacity of its members to maintain, through communication, a working consensus about the social order. It is vital insofar as an individual's ability to communicate with others (and thereby establish credibility as a relatively predictable member of the society) enhances that person's chances for survival, whereas the absence of this ability is generally regarded as a serious form of personal pathology, requiring social control. Occasionally, children have been discovered who, having spent their earliest years in isolation from other human beings, have lacked verbal and other modes of communication experience. These isolated children behaved in ways that would strike most of us as much "worse" than those of many animals. Not until the rudiments of human communication were established with these unfortunate children did they enter into social relations with other humans and acquire some of the cultural advantages that most persons accept as a birthright.[1]

It seems inevitable that a process so basic to human social

---

[1] For a summary of several cases of isolated human beings, see Robert M. MacIver and Charles H. Page, *Society, An Introductory Analysis* (New York: Rinehart, 1949), pp. 44–45.

survival should, in whole or in part, have been a subject for study throughout history. Indeed, from antiquity to modern times the topic of human communication has attracted the attention of a long line of authors representing a rich assortment of intellectual orientations, including the artistic, the philosophical, and the political. Only recently, however, has communication become a topic for scientific investigation, particularly, for inquiry by social scientists in the fields of anthropology, political science, social psychology, and sociology. The present work assumes a *sociological* orientation to the subject.

But the entire field of human communication is not the concern of this book. From the wide range of ways through which communication is performed in human societies, we shall focus on one especially important form, *mass communication*. This book presents a sociological analysis of the nature, process, and social consequences of mass communication.

WHAT IS MASS COMMUNICATION?

To start, we need a working definition of mass communication.[2] We shall first describe the characteristics of mass communication that help to distinguish it from other forms of human communication. Then, in a later section of this chapter, we shall

---

[2] We exclude nonsymbolic, animal "communication" from our definition because the focus of our work is on human social communication and, particularly, on mass communication. Our concept of communication is not restricted, however, to one mode (for example, written language) or to one channel (for example, auditory) of symbolic exchange. And we conceive of communication as involving more than the mechanical transmission of information between senders and receivers. Our perspective is derived from sociology, not from engineering.

One purpose of any definition is to inform the reader of the sense in which a word—which may have many meanings—is to be used as a term for purposes of the discussion that follows. A term should be regarded as a working concept rather than as a definitive statement about reality. The reader is encouraged to examine how other authors use the words "communication" and "mass communication" for their purposes. Examples can be found in any of the several anthologies cited in the Selected Readings. See also, Wilbur Schramm, *Men, Messages, and Media: A Look at Human Communication* (New York: Harper & Row, 1973); George Gerbner, "Mass Media and Human Communication Theory," in *Human Communication Theory*, ed. Frank Dance (New York: Holt, Rinehart & Winston, 1967); and Ray L. Birdwhistell, *Kinesics and Context: Essays on Body Motion Communication* (Philadelphia: University of Pennsylvania Press, 1970).

speculate about some of the social consequences of the mass form of communication.

In popular usage the phrase "mass communication" evokes images of television, radio, motion pictures, newspapers, comic books, and so on. But these technical instruments should not be mistaken for the *process* that concerns us here. "Mass communication," as it is used in this book, is not merely a synonym for communication by means of radio, television, or any other modern technique. Although modern technology is essential to the process, its presence does not always signify mass communication. The nationwide telecast of a political convention is mass communication; the closed-circuit telecast over which industrial assembly line operations are monitored by an engineer is not. Or, to take a more mundane example, a Hollywood motion picture is mass communication; a home movie of vacation scenes is not. Both media in each example use similar techniques— electronic transmission of images in one case, film recordings of scenes in the other. Nevertheless, one member of each pair does not qualify as mass communication. It is not the technical components of modern communications systems that distinguish them as mass media; rather, mass communication is a special kind of social communication involving distinctive operating conditions, primary among which are the nature of the audience, of the communication experience, and of the communicator.

Nature of the Audience

Mass communication is directed toward a relatively large, heterogeneous, and anonymous audience. Hence messages addressed to specific individuals are not customarily regarded as mass communications. Such criteria exclude letters, telephone calls, telegrams, and the like from our definition. This does not deny that the postal and telecommunications systems play an important role in the communications network of any society. Most certainly they do. Indeed, in some instances they are often linked to the mass media, performing vital functions in the overall communications process and aiding, for example, in the spread of information to areas of society or segments of the population not reached by the mass media. But the term "mass communication" is reserved for other activities.

Each of the criteria cited here for a mass audience is relative and needs further specification. For example, what size audience is "large"? Extreme cases are easily classified: a television audience of millions is large; a lecture audience of several dozen is small. But what about an audience of several hundred people listening to an evangelist speaking in a tent? Obviously the cutoff point must be an arbitrary one. We consider as "large" any audience exposed to a communication during a short period of time and of such a size that the communicator cannot interact with its members on a face-to-face basis.

The second requirement is that the audience be heterogeneous. Thus communications directed solely toward an exclusive or elite audience are excluded. For example, the transmission of news (by whatever means) exclusively to members of a governing party or ruling class is not mass communication. Mass-communicated news is offered to an aggregation of individuals occupying a variety of positions within the society—persons of many ages, of both sexes, of many levels of education, from many geographic locations, and so on.

Finally, the criterion of anonymity means that the individual members of the audience generally remain personally unknown to the communicator. This does not mean that they are socially isolated. Indeed, there is growing evidence that much of mass communication exposure takes place within the setting of small social groups; and even when physically isolated, the audience member is linked to a number of primary and secondary social groupings that can modify his or her reaction to the message. But with respect to the communicator, the message is addressed "to whom it may concern."

Nature of the Communication Experience

Mass communication may be characterized as public, rapid, and transient. It is public, not private, communication. Messages are addressed to no one in particular; their content is open for public surveillance. Members of the audience are aware that others are witnessing the same mass-communicated materials. The messages are rapid in that they are intended to reach large audiences within a relatively short time or even instantly—unlike works of fine art, which may be examined at leisure over centuries. "Transient" means that mass-communicated content is usually made to be consumed immediately, not to be entered into permanent records. Of course, there are exceptions, such as film libraries, radio transcriptions, and videotape recordings; but customarily the output of the mass media is regarded as expendable.

As we will note in more detail later, the nature of the communication experience has important social consequences. Its public character may make it a subject for community censorship and control through legislation, public opinion, and other social mechanisms. The simultaneity of the message—its ability to reach large audiences in a brief time span—suggests potential social power in its impact. The transiency of mass communication has led, in many instances, to an emphasis on timeliness, superficiality, and sensationalism in content.

Nature of the Communicator

Mass communication is organized communication. Unlike the lone artist or writer, the "communicator" in mass media works through a complex organization embodying an extensive division of labor and an accompanying degree of expense. One need only call to mind the vast organizational structure surrounding the production of a Hollywood film or the bureaucratic complexity of television network production to recognize the dissimilarities between such communication and traditional earlier forms. Program costs for children's television shows were estimated at $125,000 per broadcast hour in 1973. The weekly budget for one daily thirty-minute television network newscast may be $160,000 or more.[3]

These distinctions are not merely academic; they have important consequences for the communication process as well. The complexity of modern mass media has moved creative artists many stages away from their final product. Furthermore, huge production expenses decrease access to the media of communication for persons wishing to reach the public.

To summarize, recent technological developments have made

---

[3] William Melody, *Children's Television: The Economics of Exploitation* (New Haven, Conn.: Yale University Press, 1973), p. 136. Also Alan Pearce, *NBC News Division* (Ph.D. diss., Indiana University, 1971). And see Edward Jay Epstein, *News from Nowhere* (New York: Random House, 1973), Ch. 3. The network rate for one minute of advertising on the television program "All in the Family" was estimated at $120,000 in 1973–1974 (Source: *Advertising Age*, October 1, 1973).

possible a new form of human communication: mass communication. This new form can be distinguished from older types by the following major characteristics: it is directed toward relatively large, heterogeneous, and anonymous audiences; messages are transmitted publicly, often timed to reach most audience members simultaneously, and are transient in character; the communicator tends to be, or to operate within, a complex organization that may involve great expense. These conditions of communication have important consequences for the traditional activities that are carried out by communicators in society —some of which are considered below.[4]

FOUR MAJOR COMMUNICATION ACTIVITIES

Harold Lasswell, a political scientist who has done pioneering research in mass communication, once noted three major activities of communication specialists: (1) surveillance of the environment, (2) correlation of the parts of society in responding to the environment, and (3) transmission of the social heritage from one generation to the next.[5] Using Lasswell's categories with

---

[4] Our sociological conceptualization of mass communication obviously differs from those that regard mass communication as merely a technologically magnified form of private personal communication and from those that adopt an engineering input-channel-output model or an information system model. Our focus differs also from the "communications technological determinism" of Marshall McLuhan, which gives emphasis to the social consequences of the technological form through which communications occur. McLuhan argues that the nature of the medium— personal, print, or electronic—makes a significant difference, perhaps irrespective of the content, transforming the nature of human experience and of society. For a forceful presentation of McLuhan's views on the impact of electric technology, see Marshall McLuhan and Quentin Fiore, *The Medium is the Massage: An Inventory of Effects* (New York: Bantam, 1967), where it is argued that "the medium, or process, of our time— electric technology—is reshaping and restructuring patterns of social interdependence and every aspect of our personal life" (p. 8). For an earlier theory of communications impact on society, see Harold Innis, *The Bias of Communication* (Toronto: University of Toronto Press, 1951). For a discussion of the theoretical positions of Innis and of McLuhan, see James W. Carey, "Harold Adam Innis and Marshall McLuhan," *Antioch Review* 27 (1967): 5–39.

[5] Harold D. Lasswell, "The Structure and Function of Communication in Society," in *The Communication of Ideas*, ed. L. Bryson (New York: Harper & Brothers, 1948).

some modification and adding a fourth, entertainment, we have a classification of the major communication activities with which we are concerned.

Surveillance refers to the collection and distribution of information concerning events in the environment, both outside and within any particular society. To some extent it corresponds to what is popularly conceived as the handling of news. Acts of correlation, here, include interpretation of information about the environment and prescription for conduct in reaction to these events. These activities are popularly identified as editorial or propaganda. Transmission of the social heritage focuses on the communicating of knowledge, values, and social norms from one generation to another or from members of a group to newcomers. Commonly it is identified as educational activity. Finally, entertainment refers to communicative acts primarily intended for amusement, irrespective of an instrumental effects they might have.

At this point the reader might properly ask: What has become of the focus on *mass* communication? Surely the four activities listed above were carried on long before the invention of modern mass media. This observation is not only correct, but it also serves to bring into focus precisely the question to be raised here: What are the consequences of performing each of these four activities *by means of mass communication*? For example, what are the results of treating information about events in the environment as items of news to be distributed indiscriminately, simultaneously, and publicly to a large, heterogeneous, anonymous population? Similarly, what are the effects of handling interpretation, cultural transmission, and entertainment as mass communication activities?

SOME FUNCTIONS OF MASS COMMUNICATION

The consequences of regularized social activity have long attracted the attention of social scientists concerned with *functional analysis*. Some of the concepts developed by these theoreticians are highly useful for the present discussion.

A contemporary contributor to functional theory, Robert K. Merton, distinguishes between the consequences (functions) of a social activity and the aims or purposes behind the activity.[6] Clearly, they need not be identical. A local public health campaign may be carried on for the purpose of persuading people to come to a clinic for a checkup. While pursuing this goal, the campaign may have the unanticipated result of improving the morale of the local public health employees, whose daily work has suddenly been given public attention.[7] Merton terms consequences that are intended *manifest functions* and those that are unintended *latent functions*. He also points out that not every consequence of an activity has positive value for the social system in which it occurs or for the groups or individuals involved. Consequences that are undesirable from the point of view of the welfare of the society or its members are called *dysfunctions*. Any single act may have both functional and dysfunctional effects. The public health campaign, for instance, might also have frightened some people so much that they failed to report for a checkup lest they find some incurable ailment. Thus the campaign would have been functional insofar as it boosted employee morale and, presumably, efficiency; but it would have been dysfunctional insofar as it had the "boomerang" effect of frightening away potential patients.

Let us now speculate about some possible functions and dysfunctions of handling our four major communication activities as mass communication. Admittedly, the account will raise more questions than it answers. But it will also provide a framework within which the role of mass communication in our society may profitably be viewed.[8]

---

[6] Robert K. Merton, *Social Theory and Social Structure*, rev. ed. (Glencoe, Ill.: Free Press, 1957), Ch. 1, "Manifest and Latent Functions."

[7] An example of such an unanticipated consequence can be found in Robert O. Carlson, *The Influence of the Community and the Primary Group on the Reactions of Southern Negroes to Syphilis* (Ph.D. diss., Columbia University, 1952).

[8] The discussion and chart draw heavily and in places directly on my article "Functional Analysis and Mass Communication," *Public Opinion Quarterly* 24 (Winter 1960): 605–620, by permission of the publisher. Further discussion of research strategies and additional examples of functional analyses of mass communication are presented in my chapter "Functional Analysis and Mass Communication Revisited" in *The Uses and Gratification Approach to Mass Communication Research,* ed. Jay Blumler and Elihu Katz, Sage Annual Review of Communication Reseach, Vol. III (Beverly Hills, Calif.; Sage Publications, 1975).

By combining Merton's specification of consequences with the four major communication activities, we arrive at a framework that serves to guide the inventory. Thus schematized, the basic question now becomes:

	(1) manifest	(3) functions	
What are the	and	and	of mass-communicated
	(2) latent	(4) dysfunctions	

(5) surveillance (news)	for the	(9) society
(6) correlation (editorial activity)		(10) individual
(7) cultural transmission		(11) subgroups
(8) entertainment		(12) cultural systems?

The twelve elements in the schema can be transformed into categories in a master inventory chart that organizes many of the hypothesized and empirically discovered effects of mass communication. The essential form is illustrated in the accompanying chart, in which some hypothetical examples of effects have been inserted. A full discussion of the content of the chart cannot be undertaken here, but the method of organization will be illustrated in the following pages.

Surveillance by Mass Media

Consider what it means to a society if its members have access to a constant stream of public information about events occurring within the society and in the world at large. One positive consequence of such surveillance is that it provides warnings about imminent threats and dangers in the world—about, say, impending danger from a hurricane or from a military attack. Forewarned, the population can mobilize and avert destruction. Furthermore, insofar as the information is available to the mass of the population (rather than to a select few), warnings through mass communication may have the additional function of supporting feelings of egalitarianism within the society—everyone has had an equal chance to escape from danger. A second positive consequence is that a flow of data about the environment is instrumental to the everyday institutional needs of the society, for example, stock market activities, navigation, and air traffic.

For individuals, several functions of surveillance can be listed. First, insofar as personal welfare is linked to social welfare, the warning and instrumental functions of news also serve the indi-

PARTIAL FUNCTIONAL INVENTORY FOR MASS COMMUNICATIONS, BY SYSTEM
(Manifest and Latent Functions and Dysfunctions)

Mass-Communicated Activity: Surveillance (News)

	Society	Individual	Specific Subgroups (e.g., Political Elite)	Culture
Functions	Warning: Natural dangers; attack; war Instrumental: News essential to the economy and other institutions Ethicizing	Warning Instrumental Adds prestige: Opinion leadership Status conferral	Instrumental: Information useful to power Detects: Knowledge of subversive and deviant behavior Manages public opinion; Monitors; Controls; Legitimizes power; Status conferral	Aids cultural contact Aids cultural growth
Dysfunctions	Threatens stability: News of "better" societies Fosters panic	Anxiety; privatization; apathy; narcotization	Threatens power: News of reality; "Enemy" propaganda; Exposes	Permits cultural invasion

Mass-Communicated Activity: Correlation (Editorial Selection, Interpretation, and Prescription)			
Society	Individual	Specific Subgroups (e.g., Political Elite)	Culture
Functions Aids mobilization Impedes threats to social stability Impedes panic Agenda setting	Provides efficiency: Assimilating news Impedes: Overstimulation; anxiety; apathy; privatization Agenda setting	Helps preserve power	Impedes cultural invasion Maintains cultural consensus
Dysfunctions Increases social conformism: Impedes social change if social criticism is avoided	Weakens critical faculties Increases passivity	Increases responsibility	Impedes cultural growth

Mass-Communicated Activity: Cultural Transmission			
Society	Individual	Specific Subgroups (e.g., Political Elite)	Culture
Functions Increases social cohesion: Widens base of common norms, experiences, and so on	Aids integration: Exposure to common norms Reduces idiosyncrasy	Extends power: Another agency for socialization	Standardizes Maintains cultural consensus

PARTIAL FUNCTIONAL INVENTORY FOR MASS COMMUNICATIONS, BY SYSTEM (Continued)

Mass-Communicated Activity: Cultural Transmission

	Society	Individual	Specific Subgroups (e.g., Political Elite)	Culture
Functions (Continued)	Reduces anomie Continues socialization: Reaches adults even after they have left such institutions as school	Reduces anomia		
Dysfunctions	Augments "mass" society	Depersonalizes acts of socialization		Reduces variety of subcultures

Mass-Communicated Activity: Entertainment

	Society	Individual	Specific Subgroups (e.g., Political Elite)	Culture
Functions	Respite for masses	Respite	Extends power: Control over another area of life	
Dysfunctions	Diverts public: Avoids social action	Increases passivity Lowers "tastes" Permits escapism		Weakens aesthetics: "Popular culture"

vidual. In addition, research has identified several more personal forms of utility. For example, some years ago a group of social scientists took advantage of a local newspaper strike in New York City to study what people "missed" when they did not receive their regular newspaper. One clearly identifiable function of the newspaper for these urbanites was providing information about routine events: local radio and motion picture performances, sales by local merchants, weather forecasts, and so on. When people "missed" their daily papers, they were, in fact, missing a tool for daily living.[9]

Another function of mass-communicated news is the bestowal of prestige upon individuals who make the effort to keep themselves informed about events. Making news available to all need not mean that everyone keeps up with it. To the extent that being informed is considered important by the society, people who conform to this norm enhance their prestige within the group. Often individuals who select local news as their focus of attention emerge as local opinion leaders in their community, whereas people who turn attention to events in the society at large operate as cosmopolitan influentials.[10]

Sociologists Paul Lazarsfeld and Robert Merton suggest two other functions of mass communication that are especially applicable to mass-communicated news.[11] These are status conferral and the enforcement of social norms, ethicizing. Status conferral means that news reports about individuals often enhance their prestige. By focusing the power of the mass media upon certain people, society confers upon them a high public status—hence the premium placed upon publicity and public relations in modern society. Mass communication has an ethiciz-

9 Bernard Berelson, "What 'Missing the Newspaper' Means," in *Communications Research 1948–1949*, ed. Paul Lazarsfeld and Frank Stanton (New York: Harper & Brothers, 1949), pp. 111–129.

10 Robert K. Merton introduces the distinction between local and cosmopolitan influentials in "Patterns of Influence: A Study of Interpersonal Influence and of Communication Behavior in a Local Community," in Lazarsfeld and Stanton, *Communications Research*, pp. 180–219. Parts of this research are summarized in Chapter 4 of this book.

11 Paul Lazarsfeld and Robert K. Merton, "Mass Communication, Popular Taste and Organized Social Action," *Communication of Ideas*, ed. Lyman Bryson, pp. 95–118. Several of the ideas about the functions and dysfunctions of mass communication that are outlined in the present chapter are derived from this insightful and instructive article.

ing function when it strengthens social control over the individual members of the mass society by bringing deviant behavior into public view. Newspaper crusades, for example, publicize information on norm violation. Such facts might already have been known privately by many members of the society; but disclosure through mass communication creates the social conditions under which most people must condemn the violations and support public, rather than private, standards of morality. By this process, mass-communicated news strengthens social control in large urbanized societies where urban anonymity has weakened informal face-to-face detection and control of deviant behavior.

Surveillance through mass communication can prove dysfunctional as well as functional for society and its members. First, uncensored news about the world potentially threatens the structure of any society. For example, information about conditions and ideologies in other societies might lead to invidious comparisons with conditions at home and hence to pressures toward change. Second, uninterpreted warnings about danger in the environment sometimes lead to panic by the mass audience. Thus, in the frequently cited Orson Welles radio broadcast of an *Invasion from Mars* of more than thirty years ago, the belief by many listeners that the drama was actually a news report contributed to their panic.[12]

Dysfunctions can be identified on the individual level, too. First, data about dangers in the environment can heighten anxieties within the audience. "War nerves" are an example. Second, too much news can result in privatization, in which the individual, overwhelmed by the data brought to his or her attention, reacts by turning to private matters in life, over which a person has greater control.[13] Third, access to mass-communicated news sometimes causes apathy; having information about the world gives the individual a false sense of mastery over the environment. People may spend so much time absorbing news

---

[12] Hadley Cantril, Hazel Gaudet, and Herta Herzog, *Invasion from Mars* (Princeton, N.J.: Princeton University Press, 1940).

[13] For a discussion of the feeling of social impotence that marks privatization, see Ernst Kris and Nathan Leites, "Trends in Twentieth Century Propaganda," in *Psychoanalysis and the Social Sciences*, ed. Geza Roheim (New York: International Universities Press, 1947).

that they take little direct action; they may believe that to be an informed citizen is equivalent to being an active citizen. Lazarsfeld and Merton call this dysfunctional aspect of mass communication "narcotization."

One also can analyze functions and dysfunctions of mass-communicated news for subgroups within the society. To illustrate, such news activity might prove especially functional for a political elite insofar as the free flow of news provides information that is useful to the maintenance of power by this group. Furthermore, the publicity given to events within the society facilitates the detection of deviant and possibly subversive behavior, as well as providing an opportunity to monitor (and perhaps control) public opinion. The attention the news media give to political figures and their behavior can, in turn, enhance and legitimize their position of power, through the process of status conferral. On the other hand, mass-communicated news may prove dysfunctional to such a political group in a variety of ways. The news that reaches a mass audience may undermine or threaten the political power elite, as for instance when news of losses during wartime contradicts the leaders' claims of victory or when enemy propaganda deliberately aims at undermining the rulers' power.[14]

Finally, one can canvass the impact of mass-communicated news on culture itself. Among the possible functions here are the enrichment and variety that are introduced into a society's culture through mass-communicated information about other cultures, as well as possible growth and adaptability of culture as a result of such contacts. On the dysfunctional side, such uncontrolled news about other societies can lead to cultural invasion and weakening of the host culture.

Interpretation and Prescription by Mass Media

The chief function of interpretation and prescription is to prevent such undesirable consequences of the mass communication of news as were noted in the preceding section. The selection, evaluation, and interpretation of news—focusing on what

---

[14] Cf. Hans Speier, "Psychological Warfare Reconsidered," in *The Policy Sciences*, ed. Daniel Lerner and Harold Lasswell (Stanford, Calif.: Stanford University Press, 1951).

is most important in the environment—tend to prevent over-stimulation and overmobilization of the population. Most people are fully aware of the economy to them, in time and effort, of editorial activity. For example, in the previously cited study of what "missing" the newspaper meant to its readers, interviews revealed that people not only missed news about public events but also the evaluation and interpretation of these events that the papers ordinarily provided. Similarly, modern journalists have modified the early-twentieth-century emphasis on objective reporting of "facts." Many journalists now extend the definition of their occupational role to include the responsibility to evaluate and interpret events for the reader, that is, to events within the larger historical and social context and to evaluate the various sources from which the "facts" emerged. And whether evaluative or not, the very fact that the mass media select certain news and issues for attention has the consequence of public agenda setting, a function evidenced by research during political campaigns.[15]

Like surveillance, the activities of news interpretation and prescription for behavior, when performed as mass communica-tion, can also be dysfunctional.[16] On the level of the total society, such activities can operate to impede social change and enhance conformism insofar as the public nature of the communication limits its usefulness for social criticism. That is, since any inter-pretation critical of the existing social order is readily visible when conducted on a mass communication basis, it can be sub-jected to whatever preventive sanctions exist within the society. The sanctions need not be connected with official censorship or governmental agencies. They may be economic or unofficial, as

---

[15] For examples of research disclosing the *agenda-setting* function, see M. McCombs and D. Shaw, "The Agenda-Setting Function of the Mass Media," *Public Opinion Quarterly* 36 (Summer 1972): 176–187. See also Maxwell McCombs, "Mass Communication in Political Campaigns: Infor-mation, Gratification, and Persuasion," in Kline and Tichenor, *Mass Communication Research*, Ch. 6. For a discussion of the new sense of social responsibility of the press, see Fred Siebert, Theodore Peterson, and Wilbur Schramm, *Four Theories of the Press* (Urbana: University of Illinois Press, 1956), Ch. 3.

[16] For one instructive analysis of the effects of edited news coverage, see Warren Breed, "Mass Communication and Socio-cultural Integration," *Social Forces* 37 (1958): 109–116.

in the case of a consumer boycott against a sponsor of a television program criticizing the status quo. When great numbers of people can monitor a communication, discretion generally diverts the content from controversial topics and social criticism. Insofar as useful social change might stem from such criticism, the limitations on editorial activity via mass media prove dysfunctional for the society.

For the individual, these activities are dysfunctional if the interpretation and editing of news by mass media weakens a person's own critical faculties. When news is edited for the individual, he or she does not have to sift and sort, interpret and evaluate, the information. Everyone is free to accept or reject prefabricated views about events, as presented by the mass media. But at some point, it can be argued, the consumer of predigested ideas, opinions, and views becomes an ineffectual citizen, less capable of functioning as a rational person.

Transmission of Culture: Entertainment

A full analysis of the other two major communication activities—transmission of culture, or socialization, and entertainment—is not practicable here. Several important aspects of these activities, however, will be treated in detail throughout the book, especially in Chapters 5 and 6. At this point we shall simply raise a few questions according to the pattern of functional analysis that has been laid out in the preceding sections.

Consider what it means, for example, to society and to its individual members, to have many socialization activities—that is, the passing of culture down to the children—handled as mass communications. Does this practice unify the society by giving it a broader base of common norms, values, and collective experiences shared by its members? And, if so, to what extent? Or does a loss of subcultural variety and creativity result from the transmission of a standardized view of culture? And, if so, to what extent? One disadvantage for the individual, it may be argued, is that the mass media depersonalize the process of socialization. David Reisman notes that the moral lessons of tales told by mass media cannot be tailored to fit the capacity of the individual listener, as they might have been in face-to-face storytelling. Hence oversensitive children might make unduly harsh demands upon themselves as they internalize the unmediated cultural lessons from films, television, and other mass media.[17] (Other questions about the role of mass communication in socialization are discussed in Chapter 6.)

Consider, too, the functional and dysfunctional effects of mass entertainment, in contrast to those of individualistic, familial, or other private forms of amusement. For example, critics of popular culture argue that mass entertainment is dysfunctional insofar as it fails to raise public taste to the level that might be achieved by less extensive forms of entertainment such as the theater, classic books, or opera. At the same time, it is argued, there is a loss of quality even in the artistic materials that are mass communicated, as illustrated by a shift in emphasis from form to melody in classical music when it is broadcast.[18] This is not the place, however, to evaluate such claims about popular or mass culture.[19]

Consider, too, the consequences of presenting via mass communication that broad range of entertainment, spectator sports. The mass media, if nothing else, have vastly increased the number of individuals who witness a sporting event (or, more accurately, the event as presented by television, radio, or other medium). Some 65 million television viewers witnessed the 1972 Super Bowl game; by comparison, total personal attendance at professional football games averages about 10 million per year, with the attendance at any single game numbering in the thousands.[20] Television, perhaps more than any other medium, has affected this area of popular culture. Sociologists John Talamini and Charles Page, in a recent anthology on sports and society, remark that "the most spectacular rise of sport as mass entertainment, a post World War II development, has been largely

---

[17] David Riesman et al., *The Lonely Crowd* (New York: Doubleday, 1953), Ch. 4.

[18] Theodore W. Adorno, "A Social Critique of Radio Music," *Kenyon Review* 7 (1945): 208–217.

[19] For an analysis of mass entertainment see Harold Mendelsohn, *Mass Entertainment* (New Haven, Conn.: College and University Press, 1966). For an ingenious application of functional analysis to cultural "taste" in the mass media, see Melvin De Fleur, *Theories of Mass Communication*, 2nd ed. (New York: McKay, 1970), Ch. 8.

[20] John T. Talamini and Charles H. Page, *Sport and Society: An Anthology* (Boston: Little, Brown, 1973), p. 5; see also Ch. 8.

the product of . . . television." Commenting on the functional and dysfunctional results of the increasing dependence of organized sports on the technology of television and on advertising funds, the authors see these consequences as including,

on the one hand, higher salaries and pensions for professional athletes, geographical expansion, dividends for spectators such as instant replay and visibility of errors by officials, and improved quality of play; and, on the other hand, ruthless schedule manipulation, the conversion of athletes into ad men and salesmen, and, in boxing and baseball, the undermining of local clubs and minor league teams—with tragic effects for apprentice players and journeyman fighters.[21]

These observations illustrate some of the many possible functions and dysfunctions of mass-communicated sports for the sport itself as well as for individuals and for the society. The sociological study of sports is a relatively new specialty; investigation of the sociological implications of mass-communicated sports is a relatively unexplored, but highly promising area for research in the sociology of mass communication.

Thus far in our discussion of functional analysis we have treated each communication activity—surveillance, correlation, cultural transmission, and entertainment—as if it existed in isolation from the others. Obviously, in a total communication system any mass medium may perform any one or several of these activities, and the performance of one activity may have consequences for the others. Our concluding proposition is that many of the functions of one mass-communicated activity can be interpreted as *social mechanisms* for minimizing or counteracting the dysfunctions produced by another activity, in order to keep the system from breaking down.

To illustrate, suppose we accept the proposition that in a modern society the individual's need for surveillance must be met through the process of mass communication. At the same time, however, the mass communication features of this activity have effects on the individual that may be dysfunctional. For example, large amounts of raw news may overwhelm a person and lead to personal anxiety, apathy, or other reactions that would interfere with the ability to receive items of news about the environment that are necessary for one's normal operations.

---

[21] Ibid., pp. 417–418.

What, then, helps to prevent such dysfunctional effects of mass-communicated news from interfering with the basic functions? To some extent such dysfunctions are minimized by the practice in modern societies of handling the second communication activity—correlation—also by mass communication. Not all the events in the world are reported to the listener or reader through mass communication. There is a constant process of selection, editing, and interpretation of the news as it appears in mass-communicated form, often accompanied by prescriptions on what the individual should do about the events reported.

But even edited news can produce dysfunctions when mass-communicated; indeed, harmful effects can come from the content or nature of the information itself. News about war or international events sometimes increases personal tensions and anxiety. This, in turn, leads the individual to reduce his or her attention to the news, thereby disturbing that person's normal state of equilibrium.

It is significant that the same mass media that provide surveillance and correlation often serve as a source of entertainment in a mass society. Indeed, the entertainment aspects of events may be interspersed with or woven into the news itself, in such forms as human-interest stories, oddities in the news, scandal, gossip, details of private lives, cartoons, and comic strips. One function of mass-communicated entertainment may be to provide individuals with respite that perhaps permits them to continue to be exposed to the mass-communicated news, interpretation, and prescriptions so necessary for survival in the modern world. At present such an assertion is only conjectural. There is no reason, however, why future audience research might not bear directly upon this functional issue, especially insofar as such research illuminates the multiple uses to which the mass media are put and the varied gratifications and annoyances that people experience while getting the news.[22]

---

[22] For a most interesting and informative study of some uses of mass media, see Elihu Katz, Michael Gurevitch, and Hadassah Haas, "On the Use of the Mass Media for Important Things," *American Sociological Review* 38 (April 1973): 164–191. For an earlier discussion, see Elihu Katz, "Mass Communications Research and the Study of Popular Culture," *Studies in Public Communication* (1959): 1–6. See also McQuail, *Towards a Sociology of Mass Communications*, especially pp. 71–75.

2
mass communications as social institutions

Social communication—which involves the activities of surveillance, correlation, cultural transmission, and entertainment—is essential to society. Sociologists are more concerned with describing and understanding the regular and patterned features of social communication than its idiosyncratic and individualistic psychological aspects. Or, put differently, sociology is concerned with the institutionalized forms of social communication and with the patterns of social organization through which such communication occurs.

OVERVIEW
Mass communication (as defined in Chapter 1) is one way in which social communication has become institutionalized. Our society expects, for example, that certain news will be routinely handled through the mass media of communication so as to reach large numbers of people, from all walks of life, quickly and publicly. Social communication also can be institutionalized in other ways; for example, a society may expect that personal news about family members will be transmitted privately and kept within the family circle. The analysis of the institutional

forms of mass communication is concerned with the detection, description, and analysis of the social expectations and prescriptions surrounding mass communication production, content, distribution, exhibition, and reception or use. Sociologists look for the cultural prescriptions as to who may engage in the production, distribution, exhibition, and reception of mass communication; how these several activities should be performed; and what content ought or ought not to be communicated, according to the norms of a particular society.

Fuller appreciation and understanding of the forms of mass communication as social institutions requires a consideration of the relationship between mass communications institutions and other social institutions (government, the economic structure, the family, and so on), and a comparative analysis of mass communications institutions in other societies.

Mass communications also can be conceptualized in organizational terms. From this perspective sociologists study, among other things, the actual division of labor involved in carrying out the production, distribution, exhibition, and reception of mass communication. One may study the division of labor among these several areas or within each of them. For example: What are the patterns of authority and status in media production? Consideration is given both to the formally recognized patterns of relations among participants and to informal structural components, such as friendships. Organizational analysis of mass communications, like institutional analysis, is enriched through consideration of the connections between the communication system and other organizational components of society and through comparison with mass communication in other societies.

Although the analytical distinction between social institutions and social organization is important, it is usually difficult to distinguish the two in a descriptive account of a specific group or organization involved in the mass communication process—say, a television network, a broadcasting station, or a daily newspaper—or in a descriptive account of a society's total mass communications arrangement—referred to collectively as "the mass media." Such case studies generally gloss over the distinction between the institutional and organizational features of mass communication and treat the medium (or set of media) under analysis as a social system combining both normative and organizational features.

In its current state, most sociological description of mass communications emphasizes classification of mass communications systems according to forms of media ownership and control. Attempts have been made to develop broad typologies of mass media systems that reflect each particular society's "philosophy of social communications" (the normative element, at least as expressed through ideology) and the organizational conditions of media ownership, access, and control, whether by government, private individuals, public bodies or other entities.[1]

One example of a broad typology of mass communications systems is provided in *Four Theories of the Press*, by Fred Siebert, Theodore Peterson, and Wilbur Schramm.[2] These scholars have found it convenient to view the communications systems of the world as operating, more or less precisely, under four major theories:

1. Soviet-Communist
2. Libertarian
3. Social Responsibility
4. Authoritarian

Under the first theory, Soviet-Communist, may be grouped most of the communications systems of Communist countries, including those of the Soviet Union itself. In these countries the mass media—press, broadcasting, film—have clear and explicit mandates from the party and government as to their primary objectives. Above all, they are committed to carrying Communist theory and policy to the masses, rallying support for the party and government, and raising the general cultural level of the people. To achieve these aims, the party and government exercise relatively strict control over the media and their operation.

---

[1] For instructive attempts to provide alternatives to such broad typologies and to substitute for them theoretical frameworks for the description and analysis of mass communications systems, see Frederick W. Frey, "Communication and Development," in *Handbook of Communications*, ed. I. Pool et al. (Chicago: Rand McNally, 1973); and George Gerbner, "Institutional Pressures upon Mass Communicators," *Sociological Review Monograph* 13 (January 1969): 205–248 (University of Keele, Straffordshire).

[2] Fred Siebert, Theodore Peterson, and Wilbur Schramm. *Four Theories of the Press* (Urbana: University of Illinois Press, 1963).

The Liberatarian theory dominates the Anglo-American and many other Western countries. Emphasis is upon the freedom of the media, especially from government control, although some government regulation, restriction, and operation may be found. The third theory, Social Responsibility, is also in the Anglo-American tradition. This theory emphasizes the moral and social responsibilities of the persons and institutions that operate the mass media. Among these responsibilities are the obligations to provide the public with information and discussion on important social issues and to avoid activities harmful to the public welfare. Often the mass media in Western countries seem to operate under a mixture of these two theories, although some writers contend that there is a trend toward the Social Responsibility concept.

The last theory, Authoritarian, was characteristic of the European situation in the sixteenth and seventeenth centuries but also is characteristic of communications systems in some countries in modern times. Under this theory, the media, private or public, are clearly subordinate to the state and are restrained from expressing major criticism of the government or its officials or both. Such restraint may be achieved through a variety of methods, such as relatively strict government procedures of licensing and censorship.

ALTERNATIVE SYSTEMS OF MASS COMMUNICATION

In this chapter we examine several differing systems of mass communication. Examples will be drawn mainly from the field of broadcasting, and occasionally from other media. We consider first the Soviet system, then, briefly, the Communist Chinese. Next we discuss the British, Canadian, and American systems and, finally, selected characteristics of communication in nonindustrial countries.

A word of warning: our purpose is not to judge one communication system as better or more desirable than another. From the perspective of functional analysis, however, the reader may discover that some of the organizational features described appear to be useful for the maintenance of the social systems within which they operate; other features, and even the same ones, may appear dysfunctional for the society and its citizens. We make no overall evaluation here of the net balance of functional and dysfunctional elements of each communications system, for such a task is beyond the objectives and resources of this work. Our approach in this chapter is primarily descriptive and occasionally analytical.

Our cases have been selected for their intrinsic interest and for their value as sociological examples. Although we have tried . to make the descriptions as current as possible, certain of the specific features (and certainly detailed statistics) will have changed by the time these accounts reach the reader. Fuller accounts can be obtained from sources cited in the references, and current events require the reader to consult newspapers, magazines, or other contemporary sources for up-to-the-minute descriptions. On occasion good examples of sociologically interesting features of a communications system, valid in their day but now having passed into history, are cited. We hope that comparative information about a variety of communications systems will provide readers with a broader framework within which they can view and understand the more familiar American forms of mass communications.

Case 1 □ Mass Communication in the Soviet Union

Of all the mass communications systems in the world, probably the most intriguing for American readers, because it contrasts so sharply with their own, is found in the Soviet Union. The major outlines of this system have been analyzed by Alex Inkeles in *Public Opinion in Soviet Russia* and in *Social Change in Soviet Russia*, by James W. Markham in *Voices of the Red Giants*, by Walter B. Emery in *National and International Systems of Broadcasting*, and, most recently, by Gàyle Hollander in *Soviet Political Indoctrination.*[3] These works provide the major

---

[3] Alex Inkeles, *Public Opinion in Soviet Russia: A Study in Mass Persuasion* (Cambridge, Mass.: Harvard University Press, 1951) and *Social Change in Soviet Russia* (Cambridge, Mass.: Harvard University Press, 1968). James W. Markham, *Voices of the Red Giants* (Ames: Iowa State University Press, 1967). Walter B. Emery, *National and International Systems of Broadcasting* (East Lansing: Michigan State University Press, 1969), Ch. 22. (As the title suggests, the Emery work provides useful information about systems of broadcasting in many countries in addition to the Soviet Union.) Gayle D. Hollander, *Soviet Political Indoctrination: Developments in Mass Media and Propaganda Since Stalin* (New York: Praeger, 1972).

sources for the information given in the following sections. We consider, first, the Soviet systems of radio and television broadcasting and then the Soviet press.

Broadcasting   The Soviet medium that contrasts most dramatically with the American system is radio broadcasting. A description of this system best begins with the unit closest to the citizen: the radio receiver. In the beginning of the 1970s there were approximately 100 million radio receivers in the USSR, or one for every two or three persons.[4] Some of these receivers (more than half, according to estimates reported by Emery for the late 1960s) resemble the radios familiar to Americans—that is, sets capable of receiving broadcasts directly from the air. The other receivers are *wired* sets, comparable to loudspeakers, which can receive only broadcasts that are distributed through a network of wires and wired speakers, called a *radio-diffusion exchange*.

The radio-diffusion exchange operates a regular receiver that picks up a broadcast in the same manner as the American's radio set and then sends it over wires to the loudspeakers (wired sets) of its subscribers. Often either the wired sets or public-address systems are located in public places—recreation halls, factory shops, collective farms, reading rooms—and radio listening thus becomes a group experience. In such public settings it is possible for local representatives of the Communist party to "agitate" the audience by interpreting and commenting upon the broadcast and by leading group discussions.

Each radio-diffusion exchange is part of the lower level of Soviet broadcasting. There are two levels above it: the local and the central. Under special conditions the radio-diffusion exchange may originate its own programs or announcements, but for the most part its service consists of distributing the programs broadcast by the local and central stations. Local broadcasting refers to the network of regional stations that supply the several territories and republics of the Soviet Union. Unlike the lower,

---

[4] See UNESCO, *Statistical Yearbook, 1972* (Louvain, Belgium: Unesco, 1973). See also Emery, *National and International Systems of Broadcasting,* p. 386.

radio-diffusion exchanges, local stations often create their own programs. For a sizeable portion of their broadcast time, however, they function as part of zonal or national networks, usually rebroadcasting programs originating at the central broadcasting level. Central broadcasting comes from Moscow. It consists primarily of all-union programs, that is, broadcasts directed to all citizens in the Soviet Union, plus special programs for selected audiences, outlying areas, and so on. These three levels of broadcasting—central, local, and lower—provide a network of radio service that transmits in more than eighty-five languages and that reaches citizens scattered over a country covering more than 8 million square miles.

How is this vast network controlled? Each of the three organizational levels of broacasting is ultimately responsible to the USSR Council of Ministers' Union-Republic State Committee on Radio and Television (previously called the All-Union Radio Committee). The State Committee organizes, plans, and directs radio broadcasting in the USSR. Within the State Committee are units responsible for foreign broadcasting, central broadcasting, and local broadcasting. The Administration of Central Broadcasting, one such unit, plans, organizes, and executes all national programs originating in the Moscow stations. In 1968 these included four simultaneous programs relayed throughout the country. The Administration of Local Broadcasting, another unit, supervises broadcasting by radio committees within the various republics, regions, territories, and large cities other than Moscow. It also supervises broadcasting by directors of the radio-diffusion exchanges. For local broadcasting, local radio committees are responsible for rebroadcasting the central programs and planning and broadcasting their own programs. These local radio committees are defined as the "local organs" of the State Committee, and their chairmen are "representatives" or "authorized agents" of that Committee.[5] Most of these local committees include a department of lower broadcasting, which exercises control over the work of the radio-diffusion exchanges in their own area. The radio-diffusion exchanges generally are managed by "editors," but some (usually those exchanges permitted to originate their

---

[5] Inkeles, *Public Opinion in Soviet Russia*, p. 230.

own programs) operate under the direction of "editorial boards." Both the editors and editorial boards are under the ultimate authority of the State Committee. The actual operation of the exchanges, however, may be an enterprise of such public agencies as the Ministry of Communications, the All-Union Central Committee of Trade Unions, or the Ministry of Agriculture and Ministry of State Farms; or it may be run by municipal authorities or local organizations. In this way, the overall structure of radio broadcasting is highly centralized, with maximum authority located in the State Committee, lesser authority and responsibility held by the various local committees, and the least authoriy exercised by the radio-diffusion exchanges that supply the local listener.

Inkeles's analysis of the radio broadcasting system in the 1950s and 1960s shows how broadcasting can be effectively controlled by the Communist party through a combination of indirect and direct mechanisms. Consider, for example, the party's three chief methods of guiding Central Broadcasting. First, the party issued decisions criticizing the work of the State (then, All-Union) Committee and directing its future activity. Such directives were customarily issued by the party's Central Committee, through its Propaganda Department. Second, the party placed trusted officials in positions of responsibility and control on the Broadcasting Committee. Third, the rank-and-file employees of the communications system included a large number of party members, who took care that the system operated in line with the party's directives and who reported any deviations to their party cells. On the local and lower levels of broadcasting, similar controls existed. Thus the local radio committees were supervised by local party organizations, and the "editors" of lower radio-diffusion exchanges were supervised by such local party organs as local trade-union committees.

How did the Soviet wired diffusion arrangement come about? What are its functions and dysfunctions for Soviet society? Inkeles summarizes four arguments that are commonly given to support the arrangement and that also provide clues as to its origin and current functions. Initially, the system provided an economical solution to the problem of communicating over a large land area to a population with limited financial and technical resources. The cost to install and operate a simple wired speaker was less than one-tenth that of a regular receiver. In addition, the supply of parts required was much less.[6] At the same time, the wired system provided higher quality reception than regular sets because the single lower-level receiver that served many wired speakers was of higher quality than the usual private set. Furthermore, it is argued that the wired network facilitates local communications and permits such communication to continue without enemy detection during war. Finally, the restriction of listeners to one program or at best a few programs offered on their sets enhances the control and propagandistic power of the system, virtually eliminating the reception of outside propaganda.

The organization and control of Soviet television appears to be similar to that of radio broadcasting, except that there is no extensive lower level of wired diffusion. In 1971 there were more than 39 million television receivers in the Soviet Union. Television programs originated from any of more than one hundred television stations and were further distributed through a number of relay stations. Central Broadcasting studios are in Moscow and are linked into a network that serves the larger area of European Russia. Many other urban centers also have television stations.[7]

The major features of the Soviet broadcasting system—wired

---

[6] See Inkeles, *Public Opinion in Soviet Russia*, pp. 243–244. Data on the initial cost of receivers is provided in an earlier essay by Inkeles, "Domestic Broadcasting in the U.S.S.R.," in *Communications Research 1948–1949*, ed. Paul Lazarsfeld and Frank Stanton (New York: Harper & Brothers, 1949), pp. 223–293. Emery has pointed out, however, that because maintenance of wired systems is becoming increasingly expensive and because the reception quality of wired loudspeakers is low, future development of facilities will probably concentrate on multiple-channel broadcasting and on improved radio sets. This new emphasis can be seen in the changing proportion of radio sets to wired loudspeakers from 1958 to the present time. In 1958 there was approximately one private radio set to every three loudspeakers. By the end of the 1960s, there was a little over one private set for every loudspeaker, and over one-half of these private radio sets are equipped for shortwave reception. See Emery, *National and International Systems of Broadcasting*, p. 386. For details of an attempt to intensify wired broadcasting in the late 1960s, see Hollander, *Soviet Political Indoctrination*, pp. 101–102.

[7] Markham, *Voices of the Red Giants*, pp. 116–117; see also UNESCO, *Statistical Yearbook, 1972*, and Hollander, *Soviet Political Indoctrination*, pp. 102–103.

speakers in radio-diffusion exchanges, levels of broadcasting, collective radio listening, public-address systems—may be regarded as products of the social history of broadcasting in that society. That is, they represent a functional organizational pattern (not necessarily the only possible pattern) that developed historically to meet the particular technical, economic, social, and political conditions of the moment: "the great distances to be covered in the Soviet Union, the limited number of broadcasting stations available, and the difficulties of producing a sufficient number of regular radio sets to meet the needs of the population."[8] Furthermore, the pattern is highly compatible with the social and political ideology that directs all mass communication in the Soviet to aid the Communist party in its education of the masses in Bolshevism, a concept of leadership early emphasized by Lenin. According to Leninist philosophy, the party has, among other objectives, the clear duty to lead the proletariat—to raise their general cultural level and to guide them toward their social, economic, and political destiny. Under this philosophy, the radio and other mass media are regarded primarily as instruments for achieving the party's goals.[9]

Soviet Press   No newspapers in the Soviet Union are privately owned. They are published by the Communist party, the government, or such public associations as trade-union organizations, sports clubs, youth organizations, factory groups, and collective farms. In general, the press consists of papers published at various "levels" that correspond to the major administrative-territorial divisions within the Soviet Union. The press is also specialized along a number of functional lines. Geographically, the levels of the press include: the central all-union press, which circulates throughout the Soviet Union; the provincial press, including the republican, territorial, and regional papers; the local press, including the district, city, and lower (primary) press; and single-copy typewritten or handwritten "wall" newspapers, tacked on bulletin boards in factories, farm buildings, and the like. The number of papers published increases as you move

---

[8] Inkeles, "Domestic Broadcasting in the U.S.S.R.," p. 256.
[9] For a discussion of the impact of Lenin's theories on mass communication, see Inkeles, *Public Opinion in Soviet Russia*, especially Chs. 1 and 2.

from the level of the all-union papers, through the provincial sector, the local sector, to the several hundred thousand wall newspapers. Daily newspapers totaled about 650 in 1971, with a circulation of nearly 85 million.[10]

Each sector of the press has special roles. Thus the all-union press carries the message of the central authorities, publishes the party line, and generally provides the pattern and main source of material for all newspapers of a similar functional type in the provincial and local sectors. The provincial press translates these materials for a particular region, clarifies and discusses regional economic and political problems, and propagandizes for the party. The local press is charged with teaching the masses and translating party directives into daily life; but it may not discuss party theory or other top-level matters.

Within each of the three main sectors of the Soviet press there are papers designed specifically to treat a particular subject matter or to reach a special audience. Among these special functional types are the official Communist party publications: *Pravda* at the central level, *Soviet Ukraine* at the provincial level, *Izvestiya* of the Supreme Soviets, and *Red Star* and *Soviet Fleet* of the military services. These are examples of all-union government publications. Papers written for workers have ranged, at times, from *Trud*, the publication of the All-Union Trade Union Council, to local papers such as the *Subway Shockworker* and *Autoplant Workers*. There are also special papers for the youth. Inkeles reports that in 1966 there were about 132 such special newspapers, headed by *Komsomolskaya Pravda*, which had a circulation of 6.8 million.[11]

The press is officially governed through the State Committee on the Press of the Council of Ministers. Ultimately, however,

---

[10] In 1961, for example, there were twenty-five all-union papers with an estimated circulation of 24 million, about 580 provincial papers with more than 26 million circulation, and about 9,000 local sector papers with a circulation of more than 18 million. See Markham, *Voices of the Red Giants*, p. 112. Inkeles reports that by 1964–1965 there were 7,700 newspapers in the Soviet Union (including collective farm papers) due to cutbacks in district newspaper publication as a result of the 1962 party reorganization. See Inkeles, *Social Change in Soviet Russia*, p. 277. For recent total figures on daily newspapers see UNESCO, *Statistical Yearbook*, 1972 (or later editions when available).

[11] Inkeles, *Social Change in Soviet Russia*, p. 277.

each level of the press is subject to the direction, inspection, and control of the Central Committee of the Communist party of the Soviet Union, which also confirms the appointment of editors. The Central Committee exercises its control through its Propaganda Department, which is responsible for the central, provincial, and local presses. Each level is also subject to control by the press sector of the propaganda and agitation department of the Communist party committee that operates on that level of administration. This sector nominates the editors for its level, supervises the press in that area, and reviews and criticizes the press in the next lower level. Thus the press sector of the Communist party committee in each republic would nominate the editor in that republic and supervise the press there, while reviewing and criticizing the district or city papers in its area. Each lower committee of the Communist party is ultimately responsible to the Central Committee. Each paper is also subject to review and criticism: the lower press may be criticized by the district paper, the district by the regional, the regional by the central all-union paper. The content of each newspaper also is subject to censorship by its "responsible secretary" and by its censor, who approve what is to be printed and released. Finally, cutting across all levels of the press, is the potential power of the chief official agency of censorship, the Main Administration for the Preservation of State Secrets in the Press (formerly *Glavlit*). In a system controlled by so many other means, however, centralized direct censorship of the chief newspapers perhaps plays a minor role.

Every publication must give special attention to letters written by readers stating complaints about such matters as consumer goods, repair and maintenance of housing, and public facilities. This system of *samokritika*, "self-criticism," provides the Soviet citizen with opportunities to criticize the bureaucracy. The disproportionately large staff working in departments of letters is evidence of the great attention given to this system in Soviet newspapers. Research by George Gerbner in the early 1960s, reports that *Izvestia*, the main vehicle of governmental news, employed nearly one-half its entire headquarters staff in the department of letters; *Komsomolskaya Pravda*, the daily newspaper of the Young Communist League, and *Pionerskaya Pravda*, the central organ of the Young Pioneers, also employed more

staff in their departments of letters than in any other departments.[12] Party leaders, through the institution of *samokritika*,
thus allow the population to participate in the process of social
control.

Summary   The Soviet system of mass communications emphasizes the following characteristics: (1) It is a *planned* system, in
both its formal organization and communication content. Newspapers, radio transmitters, diffusion networks, and other media
can be altered to fit the changing needs of the society by expand-
ing or contracting, by focusing on a special segment of the
audience, and so on. (2) The media are operated under a philosophy strongly committed to the Communist party line and
the achievement of Soviet goals. (3) There is a high degree of
review and control of communications content. (4) There is a
high degree of specialization, especially with respect to the level
or type of audience toward which each medium is directed. (5)
The Soviet system maximizes opportunities for audience exposure in a group context, such as listening to the radio in public
halls, reading news while gathered before the wall newspapers,
watching movies projected by rural mobile units, and visiting
reading rooms at collective farms and other places.

At the risk of oversimplification, the four major communications activities that concerned us in Chapter 1 may be ranked
as follows in the Soviet system. (1) The Soviet system gives
priority to the interpretation of events and to prescriptions for
conduct in the audience. The concept of "news" in the Soviet
press does not mean the rapid reporting of current events out
of their historical context. Rather, the Soviet editor is responsible
for selecting from the events of past and recent history those
incidents which illustrate or document the ongoing social processes, especially the process of Socialist construction. Furthermore, a large portion of the daily press is often devoted to
suggestions and instructions (in short, prescriptions) for the
conduct of local party officials, workers, and others. (2) High
priority is given also to the transmission of Soviet culture,
including culture in the broader sense of the basic values and

---

[12] See ibid., p. 278, and Gerbner, "Institutional Pressures upon Mass
Communicators," pp. 231–238.

norms of the civilization as well as culture in the sense of artistic and intellectual materials. Thus many radio broadcasts consist of music, much of it classical. (3) Entertainment receives less emphasis, except for those forms of entertainment that show maximum promise of improving the audience's taste or of contributing to its political or cultural education. (4) Surveillance or reporting of news events, as we know it, plays a less important part in the Soviet system. The mass media have not been obliged, in the past, to transmit information about current events to the audience rapidly, although there are indications that this is changing. Gayle Hollander reports that developments in Soviet radio and television news reporting had produced certain changes in the practice of mass communications in the USSR by the mid-1960s. Among these changes are an increase in the role of radio and television in the rapid transmission of information; an increase in the variety of news presentations, including information about accidents and other socially undesirable events previously reported chiefly through foreign radio or by word of mouth; and an "attempt to delineate separate functions for the news media, so that they complement, not compete with, one another."[13] These developments further illustrate the way in which mass communications comprise a system within the Soviet society—a system that is highly controlled and planned but that nevertheless must adapt to new conditions and to the needs of the society as perceived by those in power.

Case 2 □ Mass Communication in the People's Republic of China

The mass communications system in Communist China has many institutional and organizational features that are similar to those found in the Soviet system.[14]

---

[13] Gayle D. Hollander, "Developments in Soviet Radio and Television News Reporting," *Public Opinion Quarterly* 31 (1967): 359–365. Quotation is from p. 365.

[14] Except for the televised and other journalistic accounts provided during and following the historic visit to China by President Nixon in 1972, Americans have received little direct information about social conditions in mainland China since the Chinese Communist Revolution in 1949. Firsthand information about the mass media in Communist China is difficult to obtain, and available statistics are soon dated. The major structural and organizational features of the communications system, however, have

The mass media in the People's Republic of China, as in Soviet Russia, serve as major instruments for implementing the government's social and political policies and goals. The media are organized, operated, and controlled to this end. Furthermore, mass media messages often are followed by face-to-face communications in organized forums, thereby linking the mass media and personal communications into a system.[15]

Radio broadcasting in Communist China, as in the Soviet Union, combines over-the-air stations and wired-diffusion networks. Wireless broadcasts originate in the Central People's Broadcasting Station (Peking) or in any of several provincial and municipal Stations. These programs can be received directly by individuals with access to radio receivers. In addition, a third level of broadcasting through wired-diffusion networks operates in the counties and communes. These local stations diffuse the central, provincial, or municipal broadcasts through wires to individual sets and public loudspeaker systems. Wired-diffusion is especially widespread in the rural areas. Alan Liu reports that the number of wired loudspeakers increased from approximately 500 in 1949 to 6 million in 1964. Emery notes that these wired broadcasting stations rebroadcast the national and international news programs and other programs of the Central People's Broadcasting Station, thereby putting Peking directly in touch with villagers throughout China's vast territory.

In recent years, radio sets capable of receiving over-the-air broadcasts have become widely available in the urban areas. Dallas Smythe estimates that in 1972 between 80 and 90 percent of the households in Kwangchow and Wuhan had such

---

been described by scholars such as Emery, Liu, Markham, Smythe, and Yu, upon whom we rely for the following discussion. See Emery, *National and International Systems of Broadcasting;* Alan P. L. Liu, *Communications and National Integration in Communist China* (Berkeley: University of California Press, 1971); Markham, *Voices of the Red Giants;* Dallas W. Smythe, "Mass Communications and Cultural Revolution: The Experience of China," in *Communications Technology and Social Policy,* ed. George Gerbner et al. (New York: Wiley, 1973); and Frederick T. C. Yu, *Mass Persuasion in Communist China* (New York: Praeger, 1964). The quotations from Smythe are reprinted by permission of John Wiley and Sons, Inc., and the quotations from Yu, by permission of Praeger Publishers, Inc.

[15] Emery, *National and International Systems of Broadcasting,* p. 465.

receivers, and in Shanghai radio sets were generally available for purchase, many of them containing shortwave bands.[16]

Regular television broadcasting in Communist China began in 1958. Early reports indicated that the majority of television receivers were purchased by such collective associations as people's communes.[17] According to Emery, television subsequently developed under goals similar to those for radio broadcasting, that is, emphasizing education and indoctrination.[18] Smythe, reporting his firsthand observations of China in 1972, cites Shanghai telecasts as typical of the television program offerings. Telecasts there averaged two and a half hours per day, in the evenings, six days a week. Smythe reports the following typical content: news, 30 minutes; literature and art, 60 minutes; documentaries, 50 minutes; and children's programs, 15 minutes. Full-length presentations of revolutionary opera, ballet, or concerts sometimes fill the evening's entertainment fare.[19]

In broad outline the press in Communist China appears to be organized into a structure similar to that in the Soviet Union. There is differentiation along administrative or geographical lines and by various specialized functions. There are national, provincial, and district (including town and county) newspapers. At each of these levels there also may be papers managed by or directed toward specialized groups such as farmers, youth, and workers. Two features of the Chinese system are of special sociological interest: the important role of *tatzepao* at the local level and the expansive network of grass-roots "correspondents" for the press.

Tatzepao, large sheets of paper on which a slogan or message has been handwritten in large or bold characters, were reportedly first used on a large scale as a medium for propaganda in 1957.[20] These posters have subsequently become a major medium of mass communications, specializing in criticism and self-criticism. They are hung by the hundreds, thousands, and even, reportedly, hundreds of thousands on the walls and in the corridors of factories, universities, government buildings, and other

---

[16] Smythe, "Mass Communications and Cultural Revolution," p. 459.

[17] Emery, *National and International Systems of Broadcasting*, p. 476.

[18] Ibid., pp. 477–478.

[19] Smythe, "Mass Communications and Cultural Revolution," p. 451.

[20] Yu, *Mass Persuasion in Communist China*, pp. 137–142.

public places. Yu reports that there is no set form or style for *tatzepao*, which may contain slogans, cartoons, accusation letters, songs, or other content. One specific use is to criticize in public some specific person or persons for their ideological positions or their behavior. According to Frederick Yu,

That *tatzepao* should be unusually effective as a means of persuasive communications is easy to understand. In the first place, it is written by and about people whom all the readers know. In the second place, it cannot be ignored or dismissed, for it may appear on the wall of one's office or at the door of one's house.[21]

Further,

virtually everyone in China is within the reach of a *tatzepao*. Its ideological assault is at once personal and direct, and the accused must react not only correctly but also immediately. Almost everyone in Communist China today is in one way or another involved in this particular form of persuasion.[22]

Smythe, describing conditions in 1972, observes that "no description of contemporary China should omit reference to the colorful display posters and billboards on socialist construction themes, the 'big character' slogans, and the wall newspapers which are very much in use."[23]

A second feature of interest is the widespread involvement of nonprofessionals as newspaper correspondents, supplementing the work of journalists. Yu asserted in 1963, that

in Communist China, where "correctness in thinking" is now believed to be far more important in any task than technical competence, writing is no longer the monopoly of the intellectuals. . . . A "correspondent" is any man or woman, in factory or field, who writes to newspapers about his work, his economic life, his experience in political study, and the accomplishments or failures of those around him.[24]

The resulting "correspondence networks" account for the claims of various newspapers to have literally thousands of corre-

---

21 Ibid., p. 141.
22 Ibid., p. 142.
23 Smythe, "Mass Communications and Cultural Revolution," p. 454.
24 Yu, *Op. cit.*, p. 106.

spondents. Smythe, in 1972, reported that the *People's Daily* had approximately 300 correspondents in one county alone, and he estimated that there may be as many as a quarter to a half million such nonprofessional correspondents throughout China, who supply some 500 to 600 articles and reports daily to that newspaper, some at the writer's initiative, others by invitation. Smythe reported:

The tactical policy is everywhere to seek out outstanding examples of socialist construction and get amateur correspondents (who are workers or peasants) to write them. The editorial function is to select from this vast flood of reports those appropriate to the short-term strategic line of the propaganda plan . . . Finally, individual articles are selected by the editors on the basis of their profundity, vividness, and inspirational and educational quality.[25]

It should be noted that for more than fifty years the Soviet press also has utilized volunteer worker-peasant correspondents, in addition to its professional journalists.

Case 3 ☐ British Broadcasting

A third system of mass communications, that of Great Britain, operates under a philosophy quite different from those of Soviet Russia and Communist China. Mass communications in Great Britain have been described as predominantly national in audience coverage, a feature that has been attributed to the comparatively small size of the country and to the concentration of population around London and Manchester. "The average Briton," writes Winston Fletcher, "gets his news from a national newspaper, his entertainment from nationally networked television programmes; his wife listens to national radio . . . [and reads] nationally published women's magazines. When they both go out to the cinema . . . they see a nationally distributed film."[26] Media ownership and control are not centralized in a state apparatus, however. Newspapers, magazines, and films are produced and distributed as private, commercially independent ventures, as in the United States. Radio and television broadcasting, long

[25] Smythe, "Mass Communications and Cultural Revolution," p. 455.

[26] Winston Fletcher, "Britain's National Media Pattern," in *Media Sociology: A Reader*, ed. Jeremy Tunstall (Urbana: University of Illinois, 1970), p. 79.

organized as monopolies under a public corporation, now are a mixture of public and commercial operations. We shall limit our discussion to an overview of the British system of radio and television broadcasting.[27]

Radio broadcasting in Great Britain, following a brief early period of commercial operation, was placed in the hands of a public corporation, the British Broadcasting Corporation (BBC), created by a Royal Charter in 1927. Radio broadcasting was a monopoly of the BBC from 1927 to 1972, when the Sound Broadcasting Act authorized the establishment of sixty commercial radio stations. The first of these commercial radio stations, London Broadcasting, went on the air in October 1973, programing only news and current affairs. The other fifty-nine stations are expected to be local operations, presenting music, news, general features, and sports.[28]

Television broadcasting was a monopoly of the BBC until 1954. In that year the government approved the creation of the Independent Television Authority (ITA) to provide commercial television programs in addition to the public broadcasts of the BBC.

As a public corporation, the BBC has certain obligations to the government—for example, the government may require the transmittal of announcements considered important to the public—but the BBC is not owned, controlled, or operated by the government. Formally, the BBC is headed by a board of governors, appointed by the queen in council, and is operated under a director general and a professional staff. Operations are financed by licensing fees from owners of receivers and in part through other revenues. BBC transmitters supply four national

---

[27] British broadcasting has been described and analyzed by a number of authors. We draw primarily upon the following works: Emery, *National and International Systems of Broadcasting*, Ch. 5; James D. Halloran and Paul Croll, "Television Programs in Great Britain: Content and Control," in *Television and Social Behavior*, Reports and Papers, Vol. 1: Media Content and Control, ed. George Comstock and Eli Rubinstein (Washington, D.C.: U.S. Government Printing Office, 1972); and Charles Siepmann, *Radio, Television and Society* (New York: Oxford University Press, 1950), Ch. 7. See also Jeremy Tunstall, ed., *Media Sociology*.

[28] For accounts see Elkan Alan, "Commercial radio begins with an uncertain sound," *Sunday Times*, October 14, 1973, and Tim Devlin, "Sounds Commercial," *Sunday Times*, October 8, 1973.

radio networks. Radio 1 is a relatively new network and provides mostly programs of popular music. Radio 2 was formerly called the "Light Program"; its content includes chiefly popular music, sports, and frequent brief news reports. Radio 3, the former "Third Program," offers mainly "serious" music and drama, discussions, news, and educational programs. Radio 4 is the former "Home Service"; it is the most diverse in its offerings, providing music, drama, news, talks, instructional broadcasts for schools, and other services.[29] In addition, six regional stations may substitute their own programs for some of the London programs.

Technical limitations have played a considerable part in the history of broadcasting in Great Britain. Because of proximity to the Continent, the British early had to reach an international agreement concerning the broadcast frequencies they alone could use without interference. As a result, Great Britain was limited to only two broadcast frequencies with power sufficient to cover the entire nation. The license to use these two airways therefore became a matter of vital political, social, and economic consequence, and it was decided that both frequencies should be entrusted to a public corporation rather than being placed in private hands (as, indeed, British broadcasting once had been).

But technical limitations alone cannot account for the unique system of British broadcasting. This system also has been influenced by an ideological commitment made early in the history of British broadcasting, under which radio was regarded as an opportunity for the cultural improvement of a mass audience. From its vantage position of monopolistic control, the BBC was committed to a policy of balanced program service designed to facilitate the cultural enlightenment of the average listener. The three sets of programs provided since World War II—Light, Home, and Third—originally represented levels in a hierarchy of cultural quality. Listeners initially attracted to radio by the entertainment provided by the Light Program were, in time, to be drawn to the more serious material of the Home Service, and ultimately their taste could be cultivated so as to lead them to

---

[29] See Emery, *National and International Systems of Broadcasting*, pp. 100–101; and *BBC Handbook 1972* (Worcester and London: The Trinity Press).

the literary, musical, and artistic level of the Third Program. Furthermore, as time went on, it was planned to have each of the three sets of programs also raise its standards. The BBC's monopolistic control over programs promised to contribute to the realization of this educational goal. Hence technical imperatives and ideological objectives went hand-in-hand in determining the earlier monopolistic form of broadcasting in Great Britain.

Both the monopolistic position of the BBC and its program policy have had their advocates and critics over time. We cannot in this book evaluate the relative success or failure of the BBC's "cultural experiment."

BBC's monopoly on broadcasting ended, and hence the total system of broadcasting changed shape, in 1954 when, as previously noted, the government authorized a competitive, commercially financed television system, the ITA. BBC now provides two television services (BBC-1 and BBC-2) and ITA supplies the third.

Independent television in Great Britain has been described by Halloran and Croll as "a federal system made up of a nonprogram-producing Authority and fifteen program-producing companies." (In addition, there is an Independent Television News company.) They summarize ITA's tasks and responsibilities as follows:

Selecting and appointing program companies. Fifteen companies operate in ITA's fourteen areas, obtaining their revenue from the sale of advertising time and paying a rental to the ITA and a levy . . . to the Exchequer. . . .

Transmitting the programs. The ITA builds, owns and operates the transmitting stations. . . .

Controlling the program output. The creative content of the programs is the concern of the companies, but the ITA has to ensure that the output of each company provides a proper balance of information, education, and entertainment.

Controlling the advertising. To ensure that in frequency, amount, and nature advertisements accord with the Television Act and the rules and principles laid down by the Authority.[30]

Halloran and Croll state:

---

[30] Halloran and Croll, "Television Programs in Great Britain," pp. 418–419.

We have seen that the BBC is a public service institution. Independent Television would claim to be both public service and commercial. . . . It is said by those in the system that an outside investigator would be struck, not so much by the commercial character of ITV, but by the extensive powers and duties of the public authority under which it operates. The Authority is meant to be more than a watchdog; it is required to be involved in the positive processes of program planning and the formulation of program policy. . . . [It has] certain duties and obligations which the law spells out quite clearly. These legal provisions have the general effect of making the Authority answerable to public and Parliament for the content and nature of all the programs transmitted by Independent Television, no matter who produces them.[31]

The British system of broadcasting is thus a combination of public and commercial organization and is heavily influenced by national norms stressing the broadcasters' public responsibility and accountability for the nature and quality of the communications broadcast. This system developed historically without producing the high degree of political centralization and control apparent in the Communist systems described above. It differs, too, in many ways from the more commercially dominated system of American broadcasting, which is the subject of Case 5.

Case 4 □ Canadian Broadcasting

Canadian radio and television broadcasting is a combination of public and private station operations, financed through public funds and commercial advertising. In this respect it may appear to resemble the British system, just examined. But the Canadians have developed their own distinctive national system of broadcasting in response to their country's particular physical, economic, political, social, and cultural circumstances.[32]

Canadians face the problem of providing broadcast services over a vast territory, larger than the United States and more than forty times the size of Great Britain. Much of this territory is

---

[31] Ibid., p. 419.

[32] See Charles Siepmann, *Radio, Television and Society* (New York: Oxford University Press, 1950), Ch. 7; Emery, *National and International Systems of Broadcasting*, Ch. 4; and E. Austin Weir, *The Struggle for National Broadcasting in Canada* (Toronto: McClelland and Stewart, 1965).

sparsely populated; most of the population is concentrated in densely settled areas along its southern border and coastal strips. A national commitment to serve its population in all regions, plus the realization that it would not be economically practical for such service to be carried into remote and thinly populated regions if financed only by private broadcasters, has contributed to the development of dual sectors of public and private broadcasting.

A second significant feature of Canadian broadcasting is its commitment to provide regular services to both of the country's major language groups, English-speaking and French-speaking Canadians. This concern has led to the development of a dual system of English-language and French-language television and radio broadcasts and networks. In addition, Canadian broadcasting has attempted to meet the tastes and needs of its varied regional and other subcultural groups.

Third, the Canadian government is concerned with developing and maintaining Canadian program content and production talent in the face of the constant threat of cultural invasion by programs from the United States. Most Canadians live within a few hundred miles of the United States border, well within the reach of American radio and television broadcasts (the latter sometimes extended in coverage by cable television systems). Videotape and film provide additional means by which American programs can be imported.

Faced with the circumstances mentioned above, among others, many government and broadcast leaders have publicly expressed the philosophy that Canadian broadcasting should be distinctively Canadian in ownership, control, and content. Another publicly expressed view is the idea that Canadian broadcasting should be one national system, serving the needs of its society, whether it operates through public or privately owned stations, or both.[33]

Radio broadcasting in Canada was through privately owned

---

[33] See as examples, *Report on the Committee on Broadcasting, 1965* (Ottawa: Queen's Printer, 1965); Report of the Special Senate Committee on Mass Media, Vol. 1, *The Uncertain Mirror* (Ottawa: Information Canada, 1970); and Canadian Radio-Television Commission, '72–'73 *Annual Report* (Ottawa: Information Canada, 1973).

radio stations until 1932, when the government established the Canadian Radio Broadcasting Commission (CRBC). The CRBC started several new stations of its own and joined them with established private stations, to form a network of regularly scheduled Canadian broadcasting. This commission was relatively short-lived, being replaced in 1936 by the Canadian Broadcasting Corporation (CBC).

CBC was established by an act of Parliament as a public corporation responsible to a board of governors. CBC owned or leased its broadcast facilities and used them, together with privately owned stations, as outlets for its network programs. Broadcasting facilities expanded greatly over the following years, especially after World War II, so that by now most of the Canadian population is covered by radio service. By 1974, CBCs English-language AM network covered 95 percent of the population, and its French-language AM network reached 81 percent of the population. Canadians also are served by CBC FM radio broadcasts and by private AM and FM stations.[34]

Canadian television, originally established in 1952, has expanded rapidly in the past two decades. At the outset television broadcasting was a national system, with CBC responsible for production, and private stations, as well as a limited number of CBC stations, licensed as outlets. An independent commercially operated television network, CTV, was authorized in 1960. By the early 1970s there were nearly eight million television receivers in Canadian homes, servicing nearly the entire Canadian population. In 1974, the CBCs English-language television network covered 91 percent of the Canadian population, while its French network covered 95 percent of the population; the private English network, CTV Network Limited, covered 77 percent of the population, and the private French television network provided additional coverage.[35]

The organizational structure for control of both radio and television broadcasting has changed considerably over the years. Initially, the CBC, in addition to conducting its own network and station operations, served as the official regulatory agency

---

[34] Canadian Radio-Television Commission, '73–'74 *Annual Report*.
[35] Ibid.

for broadcasting, recommending licenses for the private stations, and so on. By clearly subordinating private stations to the CBC, this arrangement, according to its supporters, helped to achieve the national goal of maintaining Canadian culture and supplying programs for minorities. Stations were thus prevented from disregarding the CBC network programs and from carrying so many shows from the United States as to permit cultural invasion. Later, in 1958, a national political change led to the establishment of a new structure for control of broadcasting, the Board of Broadcast Governors, to regulate both the public and private stations and networks. The CBC was reconstituted as a separate body under its own board of directors. Still later, in 1968, new legislation established the Canadian Radio-Television Commission, replacing the Board of Broadcast Governors, strengthening the single control over both the CBC and private broadcast operations. These changes are in keeping with the concept of Canadian broadcasting as a single national system—a concept that has persisted over the years.

In its annual report for 1970–1971 the Commission asserted that:

Broadcasting is not an end in itself. It is subject to higher and more general imperatives of national development and survival. Thus broadcasting is an integral part of the larger constitutional domaine; a national priority itself, it may at certain times be subject to realignment with other national priorities, be they economic, social, political or cultural.[36]

Among these national priorities have been, as mentioned above, the extension of quality radio and television coverage to remote areas of the provinces as well as to people in the metropolises, bilingual broadcasting, and barriers against cultural invasion from the United States. Efforts to cultivate and preserve Canadian cultural content have included limitations on the ownership of broadcasting facilities by foreigners, specifications for the minimum amount of broadcast content that must be Canadian programing (including Canadian music), and regulations limiting

---

[36] Canadian Radio-Television Commission, '70–71 Annual Report (Ottawa: Information Canada, 1971), p. 3.

the amount of programing that comes from any one foreign country. Through such efforts the Canadian system strives to maintain a national cultural integrity in the face of unusual, if not unique, geographical, technical, social, and economic circumstances. It thus provides an important sociological case study in the adaption of broadcasting to a social system.

Case 5 □ American Broadcasting

No other country in the world is as permeated by mass media as is the United States. Each day over 62 million newspapers are circulated—about one copy for every three people. Over 336 million radios are available—more than one per person. Approximately 100 million television sets are in use in 96 percent or more of America's households; about a third of these households have two or more sets. And millions of magazines and comic books circulate every month.[37]

For the most part, the American media are privately owned and operate as profit-making organizations. But they are subject to some governmental regulation, especially when their operations require the use of public resources or touch upon matters of public welfare. Hence radio and television broadcasting, which make use of public airways, must be licensed by the federal government; laws prohibit the transmission of material considered libelous; censorship has been employed in time of war; and so on. Aside from such specific situational regulations, however, the American media operate chiefly as business enterprises, under a philosophy of minimum governmental restrictions.

The legal roots of the American approach toward mass communication can be found in the First Amendment to the Consti-

---

[37] It is impossible, of course, to present accurate up-to-date statistics on American media audiences, because published data are so soon out-of-date. Reasonably current figures can be obtained in yearly editions of *Statistical Abstracts* (Washington, D.C.: U.S. Government Printing Office), various publications of the U.S. Census Bureau, market research reports, and occasional national surveys such as that reported in a recent sociological analysis of television audiences, Robert T. Bower, *Television and the Public* (New York: Holt, Rinehart & Winston, 1973). See also UNESCO, *Statistical Yearbooks*.

tution, which guarantees freedom of speech and press. Each of the mass media at various times in its history has defended itself from what it regarded as excessive government control by recourse to this amendment.[38] This legal protection of the media has been substantially supported by American public opinion. For example, national polls have shown that at least 95 percent of the public say that they believe in freedom of speech.

Nevertheless, neither the law nor public opinion endorses *unlimited* freedom of expression. The norm of freedom of expression becomes qualified when it appears to conflict with certain other social values and social institutions. The courts have held that freedom of the press does not extend to the publication of obscene material or writing that constitutes a clear and present danger to the nation. Public sentiment likewise qualifies its approval of freedom. National surveys conducted by *Fortune* magazine during the 1930s showed that only about half of the public thought that newspapers should be allowed to print anything they choose except libelous matter. At that time many people felt that divorce hearings, paintings of nudes, and attacks on public officials should not be allowed in newspapers and magazines.[39] In 1970 a national survey conducted by CBS News revealed that only 42 percent of the public agreed that except in time of war, newspapers, radio, and television should have the right to report any story, even one that the government feels is harmful to our national interest.[40]

The following paragraphs examine, very briefly, the current organization of broadcasting in America, touching on the chang-

---

[38] Government officials have been very critical of the mass media at times and have attempted to restrict press and broadcast activities through appeals to public opinion and by legislation, court rulings, and other means. The Nixon administration, for example, was outspokenly critical of mass media coverage, with former Vice-President Spiro Agnew often leading the attack. Discussions of current developments can be found in such specialized publications as the *Columbia Journalism Review*.

[39] Hadley Cantril, ed., *Public Opinion 1935–1946* (Princeton, N.J.: Princeton University Press, 1951), pp. 244, 416–418.

[40] Robert Chandler, *Public Opinion: Changing Attitudes on Contemporary Political and Social Issues* (New York: Bowker 1972), p. 7. See also Hazel Erskine, "The Polls: Opinion of the News Media," *Public Opinion Quarterly* 34 (Winter 1970–1971): 630–643.

ing role of the government and some of the historic steps in the development of the present organizational structure.[41]

Current Structure of the Radio and Television Industry Anyone who intends to transmit radio or television signals within the United States must first obtain the permission of the federal government through the Federal Communications Commission (FCC), an independent government agency established by Congress in 1934. The FCC is, in its own words,

charged with regulating interstate and foreign communications by radio, television, wire and cable. It is also responsible for orderly development and operation of broadcast services, and for rapid, efficient, nationwide and worldwide telephone and telegraph service at reasonable rates. Other functions include the protection of life and property through radio, and the use of radio and television facilities to strengthen national defense. The Commission's jurisdiction covers the fifty States, Guam, Puerto Rico and the Virgin Islands.[42]

Thus the FCC is empowered, among its other charges, to issue, review, and renew licenses for broadcasting. The licenses stipulate the frequency on which broadcasters must remain, the power and times of their transmissions, and other terms of operation.

Since technical conditions limit the number of frequencies available for radio or television broadcasting, not every applicant can obtain a license. Some criteria of priority had to be developed, and a certain amount of sharing of frequencies is necessary to maximize the service provided by the available frequencies. Some radio stations can operate during certain hours of the day only, for example, when there is little chance that their signals will interfere with those of other nearby or distant stations. Other stations are given priority to operate with stronger signals and at different times in order to reach parts of the country that might not otherwise be serviced. Maximizing the public service

---

[41] There are a number of available accounts of American broadcasting. Works that have been especially useful here are: Sydney Head, *Broadcasting in America* (New York: Houghton Mifflin, 1972); Llewellyn White, *The American Radio* (Chicago: University of Chicago Press, 1947); and George Gerbner, "The Structure and Process of Television Program Content Regulation in the United States," in *Television and Social Behavior*, Vol. 1, pp. 386–414.

[42] Federal Communications Commission, *37th Annual Report/Fiscal Year 1971* (Washington, D.C.: U.S. Government Printing Office, 1971), p. xi.

performed by radio and television broadcasting is a major concern of the federal government. Hence all applicants for new licenses or renewals must demonstrate that they will operate "in the public interest, convenience, and necessity."

Because of its privileged use of a scarce public resource—that is, the airwaves—commercial broadcasting, although a business, has been regarded as a business affected with a public interest. It has, as a consequence, been subject to more direct regulation by the national government than most of the other American media. Still this control tends to be more regulatory than restrictive in its intent and effects. The FCC is forbidden by law, for example, to censor programs. But it is charged with the responsibility for determining, as noted above, that each broadcast station operates "in the public interest, convenience, and necessity."

The American system of governmental regulation of broadcasting is a complicated one of interactions between a regulative agency that has been sorely understaffed since its creation; commercial broadcast interests that, from the time of their initial role in helping to create the regulatory agency, have striven to maintain sufficient independence to protect their huge financial investments and ability to make money; and politicians, interest groups, and various other spokesmen for the public, who have urged the agency to develop and enforce regulations that each sees as essential to the public interest. Neither space nor available data permit the full exploration of this drama here. But each of these major components can be touched upon briefly, in order to provide the reader with a perspective on the complexity of the system at work and some information about how it came about.

The Shaping of the American System During the early years, radio was controlled under the Radio Act of 1912, which empowered the secretary of commerce to issue licenses specifying frequency of operation. Prior to 1922 licensees were primarily maritime stations and a few amateurs, but when broadcasting "arrived" the number of applicants increased greatly. The courts held that the secretary of commerce and labor was required to issue licenses and to assign frequencies to all applicants. But as the transmitters increased in number, they began to interfere with one another—some stations drifted from their assigned frequencies, more powerful stations blanked out weaker ones, and portable transmitters added to the confusion. Hopes for self-regulation within the industry were not realized, and members of the industry began to look to the federal government for relief from the congestion on the airways. In 1927 a new Radio Act was passed, asserting the federal government's right to regulate all forms of radio communication within the United States through a system of licensing to be administered by a Federal Radio Commission. This authority became the FCC under the Communications Act of 1934.

The financial resources of the FCC and the size of its staff are small, considering the magnitude of its public charge. The task of overseeing broadcast activities (let alone the additional responsibilities of the FCC mentioned above) is formidable. In 1972, 8,155 broadcasting stations were on the air, including 6,719 commercial radio stations, 521 educational radio stations, 701 commercial television stations, and 214 educational television stations. In addition, there were 2,839 cable television operations. Commercial broadcasting constitutes the bulk of the stations, although public and educationally operated broadcasts have increased since the enactment of the Public Broadcasting Act of 1967 and the establishment of the Corporation for Public Broadcasting in 1969.

To carry out its many tasks, the FCC, which consists of seven members, appointed by the President and confirmed by the Senate, operates with a staff of approximately 1,560 employees. Only a few hundred staff members are available for concentration on problems of broadcasting, including implementing the FCC's regulatory program, processing applications, and handling complaints and investigations. In 1972 the Commission received more than 2,874 applications for radio broadcast license renewals, 816 applications for new radio licenses, 378 requests for television broadcast license renewals, and 83 requests for new television licenses. In addition, there were large numbers of requests for transfers of licenses, television translators and signal boosters, and other broadcasting operations. The FCC also received more than 22,000 complaints from the public and from broadcasters.[43]

---

[43] These data were computed from information contained in the Federal Communications Commission, *38th Annual Report/Fiscal Year 1972* (Washington, D.C.: U.S. Government Printing Office, 1972).

"The relative scarcity of FCC resources and manpower," in the judgment of communications economist William Melody, writing in 1973, has

acted to inhibit the aggressiveness of Commission action. Monitoring functions could not be as thorough as desired; industry performance and compliance with regulatory law had to be carried out largely on the honor system, and the Commission usually awaited initiation of a complaint from other quarters before taking action. In addition, priorities had to be set in which long-range planning functions were subordinated to day-to-day administrative procedures. Policy therefore came to be formulated on an ad hoc, case-by-case basis, rather than on long-range policy goals and programs of action.[44]

Melody also notes limitations imposed by the fact that the FCC cannot directly regulate the broadcast networks; that it has a wide range of administrative responsibilities in addition to those directly dealing with broadcasting; and that the broadcast industry has taken an active role in making its own interests and desires known.

The government's concern for responsible broadcasting has been paralleled by movements within the industry itself toward greater self-regulation and toward the assumption of its public service obligations, as demonstrated in the codes of ethics for radio and television adopted by the National Association of Broadcasters. These codes not only assert the freedom of broadcasters but also underscore their responsibility to the public. Enforcement of both federal and self-imposed norms in broadcasting is complicated, however, by the structure of the industry, in which the power of program construction is sometimes assigned not only to the individual station owner-operator but also to networks, production companies, and advertising agencies.[45]

Each radio or television station is responsible for selecting the material that it broadcasts. The station originates some of this material, but many stations also carry programs distributed

---

[44] William Melody, *Children's Television: The Economics of Exploitation* (New Haven, Conn.: Yale University Press, 1973), p. 103. By permission of the publisher.

[45] For analyses of the codes and how they work in practice, see Gerbner, "The Structure and Process of Television Program Content Regulation in the United States," and Head, *Broadcasting in America.*

through one or another of the regional or national networks with which a station becomes affiliated. The networks own a few important stations of their own primarily in the major metropolitan centers, but the affiliated stations supply their greatest number of outlets. An affiliated station agrees to put aside certain broadcast hours, for which the network supplies programs. The local station may make additional hours available to the network in return for further programing supplied. The stations in the network thus created may, in fact, vary from time to time and from program to program as each of the potential members decides whether or not to "hook-in." Networks need no license, except for the stations they own and operate themselves. But networks have provided important support for codes of self-regulation within the industry.

Its revenues make the broadcasting industry a big business. In 1971 television revenues were $2,750,000,000, and radio revenues were $1,260,000,000. Together they total more than $4 billion.[46] Most of the money for stations comes through the sale of time to advertisers. On the local level a potential sponsor may deal directly with the station. On the national level, however, most advertisers deal with the networks through an advertising agency. Either directly or through an agency, advertisers may buy time for brief, "spot" announcements about their products or may sponsor particular programs. Some of these programs are created and controlled by the station itself, and some are created by the networks, by independent producers, or by advertising agencies.

Broadcasting is big business in an organizational sense, too, as conglomerate ownership links stations and networks to other media, such as newspapers, and to large diversified corporations. A brief history of one such corporation will illustrate this phenomenon.

The initial period in the history of radio may be characterized as one of great amateur inventiveness, experimentation, and unregulated growth. Then, with the promise of commercial advantages, a continuing struggle for power and control of the industry developed. Legal fights over patents for the technical

---

[46] Federal Communications Commission, *38th Annual Report.*

components and processes necessary for radio communication became "patent wars," from which a few large-scale organizations emerged to dominate the industry. In time, some of these giants formed combinations either within one branch of the industry (for example, manufacturing), between several branches of the industry (for example, manufacturing and broadcasting), or between several different mass media industries (for example, joint ownership of newspapers and radio). Occasionally, communications empires resulted, within which broadcasting was only a part. One such empire is the RCA Corporation, formerly the Radio Corporation of America.[47]

RCA was formed in 1919 to purchase the radio rights and assets of the American Marconi Company (then controlled by British Marconi). At that time commercial radio broadcasting had not yet begun, but it was subsequently developed by several organizations, including RCA. Competition became especially keen between the American Telephone and Telegraph Company and RCA. Each organization built a network of affiliated radio stations that centered around its major station in the New York City area, WEAF and WJZ respectively. In 1926, after an agreement was concluded between RCA, A.T.&T., and others, RCA emerged as the major broadcaster. RCA developed commercial broadcasting through a subsidiary organization, the National Broadcasting Company (NBC), which was later reorganized as two semi-independent networks. These were the Blue Network, centering on the old RCA network of stations affiliated with WJZ (later sold by NBC), and the Red Network, the stations affiliated with WEAF (which A.T.&T. had sold to RCA).

Within a few decades of its founding, RCA extended its operations to include many diverse communications activities. It established two subsidiaries to handle the old Marconi business—the Radiomarine Corporation of America and RCA Communications. It obtained control of the Victor Talking Machine Company and a number of other companies, permitting it eventually to expand its manufacturing of radio receivers, phonograph recordings, and

---

[47] For more detailed accounts, see White, *The American Radio*, Chs. 2 and 3; Head, *Broadcasting in America*, especially Chs. 7 and 8; and *Television Factbook Sources*, No. 42 (Washington, D.C.: Television Digest, 1973), pp. 308a–309a.

electronic parts and equipment through the RCA Victor Division. Other subsidiaries were developed for servicing electronic equipment (RCA Service), for research (RCA Laboratories), for training (RCA Institute), and for the distribution of products (RCA International Division). The organizational scope, structure, and composition of RCA have continued to change with time. By 1972 its additional subsidiaries included Random House, Inc., and the Hertz Corporation.

Hence network broadcasting, the primary function of NBC, has become, in this instance, part of a vast communications organization involved in manufacturing, distribution, sales, service, telecommunications, recording, broadcasting, training, publishing, and research. Nor is NBC unique. Other networks, notably CBS and ABC, also have organizational connections with nonbroadcasting activities.

Big business and government regulation, thus, are two of the forces shaping the American system of broadcasting. Despite the limited resources available to the FCC, and given the economic power of the industry that it is required to regulate, the FCC has made a number of historic decisions and regulations that have greatly affected the structure of the broadcasting industry and the content of its programing (for example, the fairness doctrine). Certain of these decisions appear to have been inspired by complaints or requests from nonbroadcasting groups and organizations and other spokesmen for the public interest. Although a review of these developments is not possible here, worthy of special mention are the 1969 rulings by the U.S. Supreme Court that appear not only to have strengthened the FCC's hand in holding broadcasters responsible for acting affirmatively in the public interest but also to have stressed the FCC's accountability for enforcing this. Economist Melody concludes: "The end result, combining the original congressional mandate and recent pressures to action, is a commission empowered to regulate technical, economic, and certain public-interest aspects of broadcasting, and now required to act positively to employ that regulatory power."[48] We are witnessing, it seems, another shift in the powers of government, industry, and public-interest

---

[48] Melody, *Children's Television*, p. 107.

groups that make up the complex American system of broadcasting.[49]

The full story of the social, economic, and political forces that have shaped the structure of American mass media is, of course, extremely complex; many volumes have appeared during the past twenty-five years that have treated one or another of the American media. But despite these excellent accounts, the definitive sociological history of these media has never been written. And perhaps none is possible, for it may well be that the detailed data necessary for such analysis are already lost in the unwritten social history of the past half-century.

Case 6 □ Communications in Nonindustrial Countries

Today many of the predominantly agricultural, less industrially developed countries have rather limited systems of mass communications. These systems are often operated under what has been called an "authoritarian" philosophy, which holds that the primary function of the mass media is "to support and advance the policies of the government in power; and to service the state."[50] To this end the state exercises strong control over the mass media through censorship, restrictive licenses, and so on, although the media need not be government-owned.

Limitations of space prevent a detailed description of media systems of this type. We choose, instead, to note two charac-

---

[49] To report on the American system is, as one critic put it, to write on water. No sooner was the above section written than a story appeared in the morning newspaper reporting that NBC is seeking court reversal of an FCC ruling applying the "fairness doctrine" to news programs. The case at issue is a 1972 NBC documentary program on pension funds. The FCC ruled that this documentary gave overwhelming weight to criticisms of the pension system and that these must be balanced with opinions more favorable to the private pension industry. The network's view is that the ruling violates the First Amendment and intrudes into television journalism. The ruling resulted from a complaint to the FCC from Accuracy in Media, Inc., described as "a Washington-based organization which contends that newspapers and broadcasters give a liberal slant to the news and exclude contrary views." See John P. MacKenzie, "NBC Seeks Court Reversal of FCC Ruling," *Philadelphia Inquirer*, January 5, 1974, p. 7-B. Such incidents reinforce our stated intention in this chapter not to attempt to report current events and up-to-the-minute statistics on the media, but rather to present broad outlines of media systems illustrating points of more enduring sociological interest.

[50] Siebert, Peterson, and Schramm, *Four Theories of the Press*, p. 7.

teristics of communications systems that are of special significance in nonindustrial countries, although the features also can
be found in industrial societies. These features are the extensive-
ness of group exposure to the mass media and the ubiquitous
operation of a network of word-of-mouth communications that
is often linked to the mass media.

Accurate current accounts of these media systems are difficult
to secure, and available statistics are sometimes of dubious
quality and soon out of date.[51] Nevertheless, it is apparent that
by Western standards, most of the developing nations have
media systems with an extremely low ratio of mass media outlets
to total population. Few such societies have more than six or
seven radio receivers for every hundred individuals or more
than two copies of the daily newspaper circulated for each
hundred individuals, and many have far fewer of both. But such
statistics can be deceptive if taken as measures of the size of
mass media audiences; for through group listening or reading
aloud, each radio receiver or copy of a newspaper may service
several persons and even an entire village. Research some years
ago in the Middle East revealed that many villagers listened to
the radio outside their homes—in local coffee houses, in the
houses of friends or neighbors, in schools and clubs, at work,
and elsewhere. Listening in group settings was more likely to be
the pattern for the poor than for the minority of well-to-do
citizens.[52]

The second noteworthy feature of communications systems
in developing countries, the important role of informal, interpersonal communication, especially through word of mouth,

---

[51] Some useful sources are Emery, *National and International Systems
of Broadcasting;* UNESCO, *World Communications: Press, Radio, Tele-
vision, Film* (New York: UNESCO, 1964); Wilbur Schramm et al., *The
New Media* (Paris: UNESCO, 1967). See also the three volumes entitled *Case
Studies for Planners;* Wilbur Schramm, *Mass Media and National Develop-
ment* (Stanford: Stanford University Press, 1964); and Daniel Lerner and
Wilbur Schramm, eds., *Communication and Change in the Developing
Countries* (Honolulu: East-West Center Press, 1964).

[52] *Communications Behavior and Political Attitudes in Four Arabic
Countries: A Quantitative Comparison,* mimeographed (New York: Bureau
of Applied Social Research, 1952). For a summary of parts of this study,
see Edmund de S. Brunner, "Rural Communications Behavior and Attitudes
in the Middle East," *Rural Sociology* 18 (1953): 149–155. Or see Daniel
Lerner, *The Passing of Traditional Society* (Glencoe, Ill.: Free Press, 1958).

would merit extensive study. In such countries even individuals who listen to the radio or read newspapers are likely to rely heavily on word-of-mouth communications for certain kinds of news, and they are, in turn, likely to tell others about what they've learned from the mass media.[53] The role of face-to-face communicators in the flow of information and influence in a society and their relationship to the mass media are of great sociological significance in understanding the place that mass media play in communications as a social institution. We shall return to such matters in Chapter 4, when we examine certain characteristics of mass audiences in the United States.

---

[53] See also a more recent example, I. Abu-Lughod, "The Mass Media and Egyptian Village Life," *Social Forces* 42 (1963): 97–104; and Heli de Sagasti, *Social Implications of Adult Literacy: A Study Among Migrant Women in Peru* (Ph.D. diss., University of Pennsylvania, 1972).

3

sociology of the mass communicator

Who is the communicator in mass communications? The answer is "no one." The question itself is, in fact, speciously formulated, because we tend to think about mass communications in terms taken from a popular model of human communications. Reduced to its minimum elements, this model instructs us that in order to have communication there must be a communicator, a message, some medium of transmission, and a receiver; a simple example would be a speaker, words, a telephone connection, and a listener. But, as noted earlier, the production of mass communications is an organized social activity, rarely the direct handiwork of a single creative artist. The content of mass communications is manufactured through the organized efforts of many participants, mass-produced and mass-distributed. To search for "the" communicator in such a complex operation is like looking for "the" maker of an automobile. It is tempting, especially when dissatisfied with the product, to think of personal responsibility or, at least, of corporate locus: if a car is faulty, blame Detroit designers; if television programing is inane, blame the Hollywood producer or the television network executives in New York. But such personalizing of the mass communicator cannot be taken literally. And it provides no base for the systematic sociological analysis of mass communicators. The sociological study of mass communicators has been long neglected by comparison with the research attention given to other components of the communications process, especially content and audience demographics. During the past decade, however, this topic has received more research attention, with some significant studies also having been conducted earlier.[1] Among the several sociological interests that have converged upon the study of mass communicators, we shall examine three. These are developments linking communications research to long-standing sociological concerns with occupations and professions, to analyses of complex organizations, and to the sociology of work.

OCCUPATIONS IN COMMUNICATIONS

One approach to the sociological study of mass communicators is to break down the general concept of communicator into its many specialized occupational components. Then the sociologically relevant aspects of each occupation important to the production of mass media messages can be examined. Jeremy Tunstall defines communicators as "non-clerical workers within communications organizations—people who work on the selecting, shaping and packaging of programmes, 'stories' and other messages for transmission to the ultimate audience."[2] Such a definition would include, among others, journalists, advertising agency personnel, producers and directors in broadcasting and telecasting, and editorial personnel; but it would exclude technicians as well as those primarily concerned with financial and other matters not directly involved in the production of symbolic messages. It might be argued, of course, that individuals who hold the purse strings are also important, perhaps critical, to the communication process (as are individuals in other spheres, such as those having governmental power to control communications) and therefore should be included among the

---

[1] For some recent examples of this new attention being given to the sociological analysis of the communicator in mass media organizations, see Jeremy Tunstall, ed., *Media Sociology: A Reader* (Urbana: University of Illinois Press, 1970), and Peter Halmos, ed., "The Sociology of Mass-Media Communicators," The *Sociological Review Monograph 13* (Keele: University of Keele, 1969). It is interesting to note that both these works originated with British sociologists.

[2] Tunstall, *Media Sociology*, p. 15.

occupations classified as relevant communicators. We shall for the moment, however, follow the more exclusive definition and turn our attention to studies of occupations directly relevant to the "creative" tasks of message production in mass communications organizations.

Sociologists are interested, among other things, in studying what kinds of people go into various occupations. The focus is not on the personalities of these individuals but upon their social origins, recruitment, and training for various occupational roles. What are their social-class backgrounds, racial identities, educational achievements, and other significant social features? Such information about the social patterns of occupational categories is pertinent to the study of social stratification and mobility. For example, it is useful in determining the extent to which certain types of occupations are "inherited"—that is, likely to be filled by sons or daughters of people holding the same occupation. This information bears directly on questions of social equality, such as whether blacks are as likely to be employed in certain jobs as whites are and whether women are as likely to be employed as are men. Such information is directly relevant to questions of social discrimination, regardless of the particular occupation considered. In many instances the social issue is occupational and economic opportunity, and the argument is made that the social background of the holders of jobs is irrelevant to role performance or to its consequences. But in other instances, and particularly in the case of mass communicators, an underlying assumption is that the social background of the individuals has consequences for the range and quality of performance and content, such as news coverage, dramatic themes, portrayal of minorities in television stories and advertisements, and the like.

This assumption is apparent, to cite a specific case, in one of the major recommendations to improve mass media coverage of urban affairs that was set forth by the National Advisory Commission on Civil Disorders in 1968. The Commission, in relating the media's reportage of urban civil disorders to the background of the normal news coverage of race relations in America, expressed the view that the mass media fail to report adequately on race relations and ghetto problems and that one means for correcting this oversight would be to bring more blacks into journalism and other news organizations. In 1968 fewer than 5 percent of newspaper editorial jobs in the United States were filled by blacks, and fewer than 1 percent of newspaper editors and supervisors were blacks. The Commission expressed the belief that increased employment of blacks in communications occupations would have an impact on news coverage of black activities, among other topics:

For if the media are to comprehend and then to project the Negro community, they must have the help of Negroes. If the media are to report with understanding, wisdom and sympathy on the problems of the cities and the problems of the black man—for the two are increasingly intertwined—they must employ, promote and listen to Negro journalists.[3]

A similar belief that access to key occupations in the communications field would increase the presence of minority ideas, tastes, and values in media content has been expressed by woman and minority groups in their quest for greater access to the mass media of communications, including the newly developing cable television facilities in urban areas. Research is needed, however, to determine whether or not ethnic or other minority-group status makes an individual a more effective communicator about minority affairs. Furthermore, research is needed to determine the extent to which a member of a minority group would be able, once employed in the media, to control significantly the content that the organization produces. The output of mass communications is subject to a wide diversity of institutional influences. These range from subtle social and psychological characteristics of the participants through pressures from economic and other interests within the industry; these influences also include many routinized task requirements of the daily job.[4]

---

[3] *Report of the National Advisory Commission on Civil Disorders* (New York: Bantam, 1968), p. 385.

[4] For a comparative analysis of institutional pressures upon mass communicators engaged in reporting educational news in the United States, Great Britain, France, and the Soviet Union, see George Gerbner, "Institutional Pressures Upon Mass Communicators," in Halmos, *The Sociology of Mass-Media Communicators*, pp. 205–248. Gerbner accompanies his research findings with a theoretically oriented scheme that considers the major power roles that affect mass communicators' decisions, the typical sources of this power, and the functions that such powerholders have in the institutional structure of mass communications.

A clear recognition of the importance of considering the social backgrounds and career histories of persons employed in the manufacturing of news is contained in a 1952 study of the editors of what researchers term the "prestige papers." These newspapers are "institutions which function to express the views of significant segments of the elite and to disseminate to the elite at home and abroad information and judgments needed by them to function as an elite in a great society. . . ."[5] Examples of such "prestige papers" are the *New York Times* and the Soviet *Izvestia*.

Case 1 □ The Prestige Editors

The authors of the study, *The Prestige Papers*, advance the hypothesis that the editors of such papers display, through background and through careers, certain social characteristics. Specifically, according to this hypothesis, they come from the same social circles as other members of the elite, for example, top leaders in government and business; they have educational and other attitude-forming experiences similar to those of the elite; they have careers that parallel those of other members of the elite; they maintain personal contact with members of the elite through voluntary association memberships, marriage, and other means; they keep in close contact with government and political figures; and they, themselves, acquire prestige and honor in society. To test these hypotheses, the researchers examined social data about the thirty-one editors in chief of the prestige papers in the United States, Great Britain, France, Germany, and Russia. The sample included those editors who served during the latter part of the nineteenth century and the first half of the twentieth.

Although the results of this interesting analysis are too detailed for extensive review here, it should be noted that these editors were men of notable achievements. All but one had gone to college, and the majority had gone on to graduate education. Some had won honors or scholarships in school. Most had written books on politics, economics, or history. Interestingly, in about half the cases it was impossible to determine the occu-

---

[5] Ithiel de Sola Pool et al., *The Prestige Papers* (Stanford, Calif.: Stanford University Press, 1952), p. 120. This and the following quotation are by permission of the publisher.

pation of the editor's father; in the other half, however, the fathers of most editors had been members of professions, often dealing with the creation or the manipulation of communications messages as publishers or editors. Most of the editors had spent part of their careers in government service. Most had also engaged in some profession other than journalism. Prior to moving to the top position as editor in chief, most had served what might be regarded as a relatively short "apprenticeship" in some subordinate journalistic role. On the average this consisted of about six and a half years on the prestige paper itself and perhaps two years on some other publication. The usual pattern was to admit relatively young men into the job of editor in chief and to recruit some persons from other professions, both tendencies resulting in short apprenticeships.

The authors found that in general the social background of the editors reflects the characteristics of the larger social structure. Each of the previously stated hypotheses was confirmed. The editors did come from the same social circles as other members of the elite, have similar educational and other experiences, have careers parallel to those of the elite, maintain close connections with the government, and achieve considerable prestige and many honors. The researchers summarize:

In all respects, then, the editors conform to those patterns of life which we would predict for the heads of one of the key institutions in the social structure. They fit into the type of pattern we would predict for the heads of national churches, or the heads of governments. They provide evidence in their careers for our assumption that the prestige paper has become the same kind of central social institution. The social structure of such institutions tends to reflect, each in its own way, the social structure of the society as a whole.[6]

Editors of prestige papers constitute a singular, albeit an important, occupational role in mass communications. Our knowledge about the relations between mass communicators and social structure would be greatly increased through studies of other key occupations. In fact, the authors of *The Prestige Papers* suggest that similar investigations should be made of publishers, managing or deputy editors, and editors of nonpres-

[6] Ibid., p. 140.

tige papers. Recently, a major survey was conducted of the social backgrounds, training, values, and career patterns of American journalists. Useful as such inquiries may be, however, they provide no guideline, other than common knowledge, about the relative power of the holders of such occupations to influence the content of the mass media in which they are engaged. It seems reasonable to assume that editors in chief have influence over content. But how much and in what ways?

THE COMMUNICATOR IN ORGANIZATIONAL CONTEXT

Faced with the task of analyzing the complex organizational structure of a communications medium, sociologists must chose what seem to them strategic occupations and work from there. The editor in chief in newspaper publishing is an example of such a selection. We turn now to television—another medium of communication—and a sociological examination of one key occupational role: the Hollywood television producer.

Case 2 □ The Hollywood Television Producer

The television film producer has been described as one of the most powerful forces in television, from both a creative and an executive standpoint.[7] He—or she, in a very few cases—has overall authority for major decisions in the production of dramatic television series that reach millions of American viewers during evening prime-time broadcast hours. Certainly, this is a key occupation to study if one wishes to unravel some of the sociological forces at work in determining the content of a major genre of popular culture. It is precisely for this reason that the sociologist Muriel G. Cantor selected this group for intensive study. Cantor interviewed nearly all the male "on-the-line," or working, producers of Hollywood-filmed television dramatic series during the 1967–1968 season. She supplemented these interview data with information obtained through examination of various records (such as scripts) and through direct personal observations in the studios. The main foci of the inquiry were the organizational, professional, occupational, and personal factors that influence the producer's selection of stories and his other

---

[7] Frank La Tourette, in a foreword to Muriel G. Cantor, *The Hollywood TV Producer: His Work and His Audience* (New York: Basic Books, 1971), p. vii.

major decisions affecting television content, according to his own account.

Few occupational titles fully connote the actual social roles that the jobs involve. Even the formal "job descriptions" do not convey the reality of complex activities and interactions involved in everyday job performance. Some titles are labels without significant tasks or duties attached, and, more generally, certain occupational titles are so broad that they actually cover a variety of jobs having few if any identifiable, significant activities in common. (The label "scientist," widely used as a job classification, is a title of the latter sort.) A sociological analysis of the television producer cannot take for granted that such a title even denotes a specific social role. Therefore, Cantor took care to let the respondents describe, in their own words, what it is that they do as "producers"—their specific responsibilities, duties, authority, tasks. As each producer described what he did, a common pattern emerged that outlines in broad terms the actual functions of an on-the-line producer of television drama series. The producer is in charge of story selection, both theme and content; hires the cast, directors, and writers; serves as coordinator between the film company and the television networks; has final authority for cutting and editing the filmed show; and is generally in charge of major aspects of production.

Given the roles the producer plays, it should not be surprising that this figure is regarded as one of key importance and great power in the industry. But, as Cantor demonstrates, even though the producer holds a position of relative power, he does not have autonomy:

. . . because the producer is a part of a large, complex bureaucratic organization, he does not have complete control. He is a working producer—a man in the middle between those above him in the networks and production companies and those he supervises in the production crew. As a representative of management, he must fulfill the goals of the organization. Ideally, the producer has responsibility for the creative aspects of the show, but this is always delegated authority because even when a man owns, creates, and produces his own show, the network retains the right to *final* approval of scripts, casts, and other creative and administrative matters.[8]

---

[8] Cantor, *The Hollywood TV Producer*, pp. 8–9. By permission of Basic Books, Inc.

Just how the producer's control over television content is moderated by himself and others during the course of daily work is skillfully illuminated throughout the study.

For analytical purposes, an occupational role, like any other social role, can be dissected into its many component activities. Of particular concern are activities central to the major tasks of the role and involving social interaction with other persons playing roles relevant to those tasks, that is, to members of one's *role set*.[9] Cantor divides the producer's activities into two major categories: (1) business operations and decisions and (2) actual film making with the production company or crew. She then details the key role partners with whom the producer must deal in each of these broad areas and whose own role performances set demands, constraints, expectations, or rewards or otherwise influence the producer's performance and, ultimately, the content and quality of the film that is telecast. The business activities require the producer to interact with or otherwise take into consideration, among others, various executives and representatives of the television networks, sponsors, and advertising agencies. During the actual filming of a show, the producer's key role partners—key in the sense that they are especially important in the producer's decisions about story selection and the creative process—include writers, directors, and actors.

Sometimes the producer interacted directly with others in these several roles; at other times he kept others in mind as reference groups whose values, wishes, expectations, and other considerations were relevant to his own performances. Cantor's findings strongly suggest that producers are as concerned with reactions of the "secondary" audience for their shows—which includes the network and studio executives and the production group, especially writers, directors, and actors—as with the reactions of the primary audience of television viewers. Direct contact with representative members of the viewing audience rarely or never occurs. Nevertheless, most producers have created for themselves an image of what kind of audience views their shows (or, more likely, will view their shows, since the logistics of

---

[9] For an instructive discussion of role sets and related concepts, see Robert K. Merton *Social Theory and Social Structure*, rev. ed. (Glencoe, Ill.: Free Press, 1957), pp. 368–386.

production require that a number of episodes of a series be completed long before they are broadcast and, therefore, before any direct measures of national audience response). Although the producers' views of their audiences were often limited to stereotypes of broad social characteristics and often did not match the actual audience composition subsequently revealed by audience research, many producers said that they consider the viewing audience when making decisions about the shows they produce. In practice, however, some producers appear to project their own tastes or those of their families or acquaintances as being representative of those of "the audience."

Working producers are likely to have direct contact with representatives of their "other" major audience—that is, the television network representatives—and these contacts, together with the producers' use of the network officials as a reference group, may lead to conflicts over the artistic and substantive content of the shows. Cantor notes that network controls can operate in a variety of ways. For example, a network liaison person may attend the story conference where ideas for new shows are presented and explored; the network censor must approve all scripts; and the network has final power to decide whether a show is aired through its facilities. Most producers reported that they had some conflicts with the networks about content, and more than half said that they had experienced network attempts at "interference" with story selection or content, or both, during the production of their current shows. But more than a third of the producers said they had not experienced such pressures.

Of interest is Cantor's analysis of why some producers seem to be pressured and others not and of why some comply readily with network suggestions and directives whereas others "seem to try to thwart the network directives at every opportunity and therefore are under constant pressure."[10] This analysis shows that despite the broad similarity in official and unofficial duties among producers and in general norms prescribing the conduct of this role, there is considerable latitude in how the role relationships are carried out. To be sure, some of the variation in role performances may be attributed to the personality and idio-

---

[10] Cantor, *The Hollywood TV Producer*, p. 132.

syncracies of the individual playing the role. But certain regular variations in role performance emerge when one further specifies the role of producer into several types of television producers. Cantor presents a typology of producers based upon combinations of their personal backgrounds and histories in the industry and their occupational goals and values. Three major types are identified: *film makers, writer-producers,* and *old-line producers.*

The film makers are usually college graduates who have studied in a university communications media program; they went to work in television and eventually came up through the ranks of a major studio; they regard their main task of producer as coordinating the various parts of the process of film making; they hope, upon mastering these skills and acquiring sufficient economic means, to make films to be shown in motion picture theaters. To achieve these personal goals, film makers believe that they are "using the system," rather than vice versa. Writer-producers are also likely to have attended college, perhaps majoring in English or journalism; most had been free-lance scriptwriters, and many had worked in mass media other than television. They became producers in the hope of controlling their own creative products and stories, more than they had been able to do when they were only writers. The old-line producers are less likely to have had college training directly relevant to media production; they had varied experience in other mass media; they are the most successful producers in terms of income and the ability to get their ideas and pilot shows made into television series. Continued opportunity to produce shows that are successful in attracting large mass audiences is an important, although by no means the sole, goal of the old-line producers.

Cantor reports that the film makers are the least likely of the three types of producers to have conflicts with the networks over the artistic, political, or social content of their shows. Film makers are oriented toward learning all that they can about production, are willing to postpone expression of their own creative talents until they can start new careers as independent movie makers, and are likely to share the network officials' views that television is essentially an entertainment medium that should give the mass public "what it wants."

Both the writer-producers and the old-line producers experience more conflicts with the networks. The former feel strongly that they should have control over the story content, especially as it is used to express political and social objectives. Writer-producers often engage in covert struggles with the networks, striving to maximize their control over the content without directly displeasing the networks to the degree that they would risk either cancellation of the series or their removal as producer. The old-line producers are likely to have direct conflicts with network officials, especially concerning what is likely to be successful with the audience—the story idea, for example, or the character of the hero or heroine—or over the choices of cast and director.

Cantor also reports on differences in role conflicts between each of these three types of producers and their role partners within the production crew: writers, directors, and actors.[11]

COMMUNICATION AS WORK

We have considered two approaches to the sociology of the mass communicator: (1) sociological studies of mass communicators' backgrounds and career patterns, factors that are presumed to affect their role performance and, ultimately, the communications content they produce; and (2) studies of specific occupational roles within complex communications organizations that influence the communicator's creativity. We turn now to a third line of research on occupations that has been productive, one that stresses the day-to-day demands of the job that directly affect the form, quantity, and quality of mass communication content.

Many of the initial studies of communication as work were done by former journalists and other communicators or performers who are now sociologists or mass communications researchers. These studies depict the occupational world of the communicator in terms and details not readily known to social scientists or others who have not worked in a mass communica-

---

[11] Other studies of television producers that might interest the reader are Philip Elliott's case study of the production of a British television documentary series, reported in Tunstall, *Media Sociology*, pp. 221–238; and Malcolm Warner's study of American television political news, in Halmos, *The Sociology of Mass-Media Communicators*, pp. 169–180. See also Gaye Tuchman, ed., *The TV Establishment* (Englewood Cliffs, N.J.: Prentice-Hall, 1974).

tions organization. These accounts help to shatter our preconceptions about what happens on the job and disclose some of the pressures affecting the communications output.

Warren Breed provides an insightful analysis of social control in the newsroom.[12] His study shows how reporters, whether under direct order or not (usually not), are influenced by the policy of their newspaper and by the sometimes explicit, although often implicit, norms about the content of their stories that are conveyed through their fellow reporters and supervisors in the newsroom. Breed interviewed 120 newsmen working for middle-sized newspapers. He discovered that new reporters were never formally informed as to the paper's policy. Rather, they learned this through a subtle process of socialization on the job. Among the ways by which policy became apparent to staffers were: reading their own paper and thereby discovering its characteristics in news coverage; being the recipient of editorial actions and sanctions, such as criticism and blue-penciling of stories (usually without any direct statement about the policy violated); hearing gossip; attending staff conferences; reading house organs; and directly observing the activities of the publisher or other executives and hearing their opinions expressed. Breed examined certain reasons for the staffer's conformity to a newspaper's policy, once learned. These included responsiveness to the institutional authority of the publisher and the potential sanctions for violation of policy; the staffer's feelings of obligation and esteem for his superiors on the paper; mobility aspirations; lack of conflicting group allegiances; the pleasant nature of the work activity; and the displacement of goals, whereby getting or producing "news" becomes a prime occupational value, binding staffers and executives and diverting attention from alternative goals such as enlightening or informing the readers.

Subsequent research by Lee Sigelman adds the further point that news reporters may be well aware of a newspaper's major policy and ideological stance prior to joining its staff and, given the alternatives, select the organization in which they are most likely to feel comfortable.[13] Reporters may change papers, too,

---

[12] Warren Breed, "Social Control in the News Room," *Social Forces* 33 (May 1955): 326–335.

[13] Lee Sigelman, "Reporting the News: An Organizational Analysis," *American Journal of Sociology* 79 (July 1973): 132–151.

provided there are opportunities, and may thereby leave a newspaper whose policy is unacceptable to them.

Complete conformity does not always occur, of course, and there are conflicts. Breed examines a variety of ways in which the news staffer may play the role so as to by-pass policy. And he shows how, failing that, a staffer may adopt a rationalized view ("it's only a job; take your pay and forget it").

Several studies examine how a communicator's work routines influence decisions about which of several possible events will be selected for reporting as mass-communicated news. Termed studies of "gatekeepers," such research often demonstrates that the selection of content is influenced less by the private ideological desires and tastes of the communicator than by the practical necessity to select from among competing stories within the time alloted. Such selection is guided by the communicator's awareness of what kinds of news stories are likely to fit the organization's norms regarding proper news coverage.

Walter Gieber studied the newspaper telegraph editor, the individual whose job it is to select reportable news items from the flow of press association information received. He studied sixteen Wisconsin daily newspapers receiving the Associated Press wire service. Although he found that the telegraph editors differed widely in their explanations and rationalizations of why they selected certain stories for treatment as news, there actually were no major differences in news selection among them. Their role behavior was not a simple enactment of their own ideas. Rather, Gieber concludes:

Common to all the telegraph editors were the pressures exerted by the reality of the newsroom bureaucratic structure and its operation. The most powerful factor was not the evaluative nature of news but the pressures of getting the copy into the newspaper; the telegraph editor was preoccupied with the mechanical pressures of his work rather than the social meanings and impact of the news. His personal evaluations rarely entered into his selection process; the values of his employer were an accepted part of the newsroom environment.

[He] was "task oriented"; he was concerned with goals of production, bureaucratic routine and interpersonal relations within the newsroom.[14]

---

[14] Walter Gieber, "News Is What Newspapermen Make It," in *People, Society, and Mass Communications*, ed. Lewis Dexter and David White, (New York: Free Press, 1964), pp. 173–182. Quotation is on p. 175.

Further insights into how the routine demands of work affect the performance of news reporters are provided by Gaye Tuchman's recent studies of a daily metropolitan newspaper and a local independent television station. Tuchman notes that the newspaper reporter works within a social and organizational context that every day poses many risks of failure—risks imposed by deadlines, libel suits, and reprimands or criticisms from superiors and members of the public. To be successful, he or she must write stories quickly (often being given less than a day for preparation, news gathering, and writing of the story), ably enough not to require extensive rewriting (for numerous revisions may delay publication of the newspaper, leading to a series of complications that can reduce profits), and with sufficient accuracy to protect the reputation of the newspaper and to avoid libel suits. Tuchman writes:

[E]very story entails dangers for news personnel and for the news organization. Each story potentially affects the newsmen's ability to accomplish their daily tasks, affects their standing in the eyes of their superiors, and affects the ability of the news organization to make a profit. Inasmuch as the newspaper is made of many stories, these dangers are multiplied and omnipresent.[15]

Confronted by such high risks in their daily occupations, newsmen invoke claims of objective reporting as their defense against potential criticism. But objectivity is a concept, not a phenomenon. Not every fact or statement in a news story can be independently verified for its truth. Under these circumstances newsmen follow any of a number of work strategies and practices to strengthen their claim of objectivity. Tuchman analyzes three major factors that strengthen the reporter's sense of objectivity. These involve the form in which the news is presented, its content, and the reporter's judgment, which is derived in part from interorganizational relationships. News stories are cast into particular forms that exemplify "objective" news pro-

---

[15] Gaye Tuchman, "Objectivity as Strategic Ritual: An Examination of Newsmen's Notions of Objectivity," *American Journal of Sociology* 77 (January 1972): 663–664. See also Gaye Tuchman, "Making News by Doing Work: Routinizing the Unexpected," *American Journal of Sociology* 79 (July 1973): 110–131; and "The Technology of Objectivity: Doing 'Objective' TV News Film," *Urban Life and Culture* 2 (April 1973): 3–26.

cedures as presentation of conflicting possibilities, presentation of supporting evidence, use of quotation marks, and structuring information in a sequence of decreasing importance. Content may be classified so as to separate news analysis and features from straight "objective" news stories. The news reporters' judgment as to what constitutes straight and important news may be influenced by their knowledge about how potential news sources, especially representatives of social institutions and organizations, work. This preconception of social reality, plus their "common sense," contributes to journalists' news judgment, which, in turn, affects their decisions as to whether or not an event, "fact," claim, or other item should be accepted and reported as news.

Tuchman characterizes these common news procedures as "strategic rituals," developed to protect working communicators (and their organizations) from blame. Hence objectivity is transformed from a subjective concept into a set of normative work practices. In televised news films, according to Tuchman's research, a number of conventions about visual presentation have come to be regarded by newsmen as exemplifying cinematic objectivity. Among these are the time convention—shoot a constant number of frames per second—and the placement convention—place the camera as though it were a person of average height meeting another person of average height. Deviations from these conventions are regarded as distortations or mistakes in television news films. Deliberate violation of these practices is reserved for nonobjective "feature" stories.

CONCLUDING NOTE

Our several examples of sociological research on the mass communicator, and especially the studies cited on communication as work, could mistakenly be construed as focusing on communicators as persons—as newspaper reporters, television news reporters, television producers. The data do consist of information obtained from individuals through personal interviews or through observations of their activities. Nevertheless, the sociological analyses are not about individual communicators. The researchers were not reporting on the private, idiosyncratic actions of speakers and writers, nor on their personalities, their creative abilities, or their personal intentions to "communicate."

Rather, the analytical perspective is on communicators in context—the context being the complex organizational structure of the mass media industry and the focus being their part in this structure as they play out their occupational roles.

Much of our knowledge about mass communicators comes from depictive accounts: novels, biographies, histories, and journalistic reports about the mass media, which describe representative persons of power and influence in them and give the "inside story" of how things operate. Useful as these personalized accounts are, they are not to be mistaken for sociological analyses, which they were never intended to be. They may, of course, constitute data for analysis or provide useful insights into sociological phenomona.

We need and should welcome additional narrative, depictive accounts of the world of the mass communicator. Even more instructive, however, would be further sociographic accounts of the mass communicator's roles and sociological analyses of how these roles affect the content of our mass media.[16] The studies conducted by Breed, Cantor, and Tuchman, among others, demonstrate the importance, feasibility, and fruitfulness of a sociological examination of the mass communicator.[17]

From such sociological investigations we learn much about how major roles in the complex organizations of the mass media influence the final content, conditions under which these influences are strengthened or weakened, the processes by which they are exercised, variability in actual role performance, some of the

---

[16] For additional clarification of the nature of depictive, sociographic, and social theoretical analyses of social roles see Robert K. Merton and Elinor Barber, "Sociological Ambivalence," in *Sociological Theory, Values, and Sociocultural Change*, ed. Edward A. Tiryakian (New York: Free Press, 1963), pp. 91–120, but especially pp. 99–105.

[17] An example of this approach applied to musicians working in the mass media is provided by Robert Faulkner, *Hollywood Studio Musicians: Their Work and Careers in the Recording Industry* (Chicago: Aldine-Atherton, 1971). Faulkner's analysis proposes that "much of the behavior of creative and performing artists in mass media setting can be viewed as *work*. They write, perform, and produce in highly organized teams that demand coordination; they face routine work pressures, try to handle mistakes at work, control the activities of colleagues, and cope with the risks of personal failure" (p. 5). Faulkner documents these points through detailed interviews with seventy-three successful Hollywood studio musicians, free-lance artists, many of whom had prior successful careers as musicians with symphony orchestras or jazz and big bands.

bers of the mass. They are usually physically separated from one another, and being anonymous, do not have the opportunity to mill as
do the members of the crowd. Fourth, the mass is *very loosely organized* and is not able to act with the concertedness or unity that
marks the crowd.[1]

The reader will note that if this concept of the mass is applied
to audience members, they will be regarded not only as heterogeneous but also as anonymous and isolated from one another.
In short, they are like separate atoms that together comprise
the whole—the mass audience.

Usually accompanying this concept of a mass audience is an
image of the communications media as acting directly upon
individual audience members—reaching each member or not,
influencing him or her directly or not. This view of mass communication has been called the "hypodermic needle model":
each audience member in the mass audience is personally and
directly "stuck" by the medium's message.[2] Once the message
has stuck someone, it may or may not have influence, depending
on whether or not it is potent enough to "take."

Both the concept of a mass audience and the hypodermic
needle model of the communication process have been modified
by sociological research. A conception of the audience has
emerged in which greater notice is taken of the social context
within which each audience member operates. An individual
(although personally unknown to the communicator) is rarely
genuinely anonymous in his or her social environment. Ordinarily, everyone is a member of a network of primary and secondary groupings—family, friendship groups, occupational
circles, and so on—which influence one's opinions and attitudes.
Inevitably, these groups affect the way in which each of us is
exposed to mass communication, how we interpret or react to
any specific communication, and the extent to which we will or

---

[1] Herbert Blumer, "Collective Behavior," in *Principles of Sociology*, ed.
Alfred McClung Lee (New York: Barnes & Noble, 1946), pp. 185–186. By
permission of the publisher, Harper & Row (Barnes & Noble Books Div.).
Emphasis supplied.

[2] For a fuller discussion of these earlier models of communication, see
Elihu Katz and Paul Lazarsfeld, *Personal Influence: The Part Played by
People in the Flow of Mass Communications* (Glencoe, Ill.: Free Press,
1955), Chs. 1 and 2.

can modify our behavior in compliance with the message.

Illustrative of the research in this area is the earlier work of sociologists Matilda and John Riley involving exploratory experiments on the effect of peer-group membership on communications behavior. They found that children who were well-integrated members of their peer groups had less preference for radio and television shows of action and violence than had other children. They also were more likely to interpret the content of such action programs in terms of their social utility for advancing the play activity of their group than the children who were not integrated peer-group members. Less well-integrated children were more likely to prefer these action stories and to dwell upon the literal interpretation of the message (for example, as creepy or scary).[3] Here is one of the many examples of the fact that the social pattern within which the individual audience member interacts affects both selection and response to mass communication.

Research has also revealed that in many instances the members of an audience are, at the very moment of exposure, participating in a group experience. We have already noted this characteristic of audiences in the Soviet Union, where group listening to the radio is quite common. But there are parallels in other societies. For example, going to the movies in the United States is often likely to be a group experience.[4] Again, the non-anonymous, social nature of the situation may affect the audience's response.

Finally, the individual's social connections provide him or her with a communication network, on a personal face-to-face basis. This informal network often gives a person indirect access to mass communication material not received directly. There is growing evidence, in fact, to support the hypothesis that mass communications messages do not always reach all members of their ultimate audience directly, as the hypodermic needle model assumes. Sometimes mass communication is a multistep process, whereby the message first reaches *opinion leaders*, or *influentials*,

---

[3] Matilda Riley and John Riley, "A Sociological Approach to Communications Research," *Public Opinion Quarterly* 15 (Fall 1951): 445–460.

[4] For examples of early research, see Leo Handel, *Hollywood Looks at Its Audience* (Urbana: University of Illinois Press, 1950), pp. 113–115.

who in turn either pass the message on by word of mouth to persons who consult them or utilize the message in the advice or information that they pass on within their circle of influence.

INFORMAL COMMUNICATION AND THE MASS AUDIENCE

Certain sociological studies, some of which are summarized below, contain information on mass communication as *social process*. First, we shall discuss three pioneer studies of opinion leaders and the linkage of these leaders with the mass media. The analyses of opinion leaders and the two-step flow of communications presented here are based primarily on studies of American audiences. There has been some research on these topics in other societies, but the most extensive work has been done in the United States. The extent to which the American pattern can be generalized to other groups is as yet unknown. Even within our own society there is much still to be learned about the *conditions* under which the two-step flow operates—how prevalent it is among various minority groups, at different age levels, and in times of historical crisis. We shall then examine selected recent research on opinion leaders. Finally, we shall review research on the diffusion of innovations, news, or information within a community and again highlight the connections between personal communication and mass communication in the total communication process.

Case 1 □ Opinion Leaders in an Election Campaign

The earliest sociological recognition of the importance of individuals in mediating between the mass media and the general public was part of a pioneering study of voting behavior conducted by Paul Lazarsfeld and his colleagues during the Presidential campaign of 1940.[5] A review of some of the background of this study provides perspective on subsequent research on opinion leaders.

These researchers were primarily interested in discovering how and why people decide to vote as they do. In exploring this

---

[5] Paul Lazarsfeld, Bernard Berelson, and H. Gaudet, *The People's Choice* (New York: Columbia University Press, 1948). Since all the findings summarized in this section are derived from this work, specific page references will be cited only for direct quotations from the study.

problem, Lazarsfeld and his colleagues introduced a new research method, the *panel technique,* by which the same people were repeatedly interviewed over an extended period of time. The panel technique represented an innovation in public opinion research, for among other things it permitted the researcher to study the *development* and *change* in opinions and attitudes on the spot. Persons who changed their minds could be detected almost at the moment of change, and then the factors leading to the change or to stability could be studied intensively. In this instance the study consisted primarily, although not entirely, of interviews with a core panel of 600 persons in Erie County, Ohio, who were interviewed once each month from May to November—that is, just prior to and throughout the election campaign.

The researchers were also interested in determining the impact of the political campaign itself, including its mass media components, upon changes in voting intention. To their surprise (for most persons would have predicted the opposite), there was very little evidence to indicate that the campaign directly influenced changes in people's votes. This is not to say that the campaign had no effect whatsoever or that on occasion it did not convert voters. But the basic impact of the mass campaign was to reinforce the original voting intention of some citizens and to activate latent predispositions of others.

The tendency of the campaign to reinforce existing political preferences can be partially understood from data on the patterns of exposure to communication during the campaign. People were very *selective,* tending to pay attention to those materials that reflected their original predispositions. Republicans were more likely to expose themselves to Republican campaign messages and to media supporting their party than they were to heed the Democratic side of the campaign, and vice versa.

The reinforcement effect can be understood also in terms of the political homogeneity of social groups. The study showed repeatedly that people voted "in groups" in the sense that persons belonging to the same church, family, social clubs, and similar institutionalized groups tended to vote alike. Of course, the tendency toward political homogeneity of social groups can be partially explained by the fact that people living under similar social and economic conditions are likely to share similar needs and interests and to interpret their experiences in similar political terms. But a fuller explanation must also take into account the political importance within these groups of personal influence through face-to-face communication. The researchers noted that "whenever the respondents were asked to report on their recent exposure to campaign communications of all kinds, political discussions were mentioned more frequently than exposure to radio or print."[6] It was in the discovery and analysis of such effective personal contacts that the concept of opinion leader and a new hypothesis—the two-step flow hypothesis—developed.

In its most general form, the phrase "opinion leaders" refers to individuals who, through day-to-day personal contacts, influence others in matters of decision and opinion formation. Opinion leaders are not necessarily the formal leaders of the community or persons holding positions usually accorded social prestige. Each stratum of society seems rather to have its own group of opinion leaders. In the study under consideration, for example, political opinion leaders were found among all occupational levels represented in the sample.

How, then, is the researcher able to identify or recognize opinion leaders? That is a more complicated and difficult problem than it might seem at first glance, yet it had to be solved before information could be gathered on the connection between opinion leaders and mass communication. It might seem that opinion leaders would be identified simply by asking people to whom they turn for advice or help in making up their minds on various issues. In practice, however, this procedure has a major drawback, for it assumes that all, or a representative group, of the opinion leaders so identified by respondents are available for study. In small communities or "closed societies" (such as residence colleges) this procedure might be feasible. But for studies in which social research must be based upon small representative samples of larger populations, the method is no longer practicable. For it would turn up names of opinion leaders who could not be reached because they were not included within the sample; and conversely, many other opinion leaders might go undetected if the people whom they influenced were not also in the

---

[6] Ibid., p. 150. The quotations from this work are by permission of the publisher, Columbia University Press.

sample to identify them. What was required was some way to identify the opinion leaders among the people about whom the most information had been and could be collected—namely, those already in the sample. If properly drawn, a sample is a good cross section of the community, from which reliable generalizations can be made.

A workable solution to this problem rests on the ability of opinion leaders within a sample to *identify themselves* for the researcher. This is not to say that they would name themselves "opinion leaders" or "influentials"; nor does it even imply self-consciousness or awareness of their leadership role. Rather, since the concept of opinion leadership refers to behavior, it means simply that these people are able to report whether or not they have been asked for advice or have given their advice to someone. From the respondents' own reports the researcher is able to specify the opinion leaders.

Thus, near the middle of the election campaign, each member of the panel was asked two questions: (1) "Have you tried to convince anyone of your political ideas recently?" and (2) "Has anyone asked your advice on a political question recently?" For the purposes of the study, anyone who answered "yes" to either or both of these questions was a self-designated opinion leader. Ancillary information and observations were obtained to support the validity of the identifications, but the key classification rested upon these two personal reports on behavior.[7]

Because the voting study was well under way before the full importance of opinion leaders was discovered, intensive analysis of their characteristics and role was not possible. However, this investigation provided some suggestive evidence about opinion leaders and set the stage for subsequent studies of personal influence. First, as noted above, opinion leadership was found to be distributed throughout the social structure, suggesting that personal influence flows not only from "top to bottom" within the society but also horizontally within social classes or other status groups. Second, the opinion leaders were found to be especially alert, interested, and active politically. For example, six of every ten leaders said they had a great deal of interest in the current election, in contrast with only one of every four nonleaders.

---

[7] Ibid., p. 50.

Third, and especially significant from our point of view, opinion leaders were more fully exposed to the mass media campaign than were nonleaders. Opinion leaders were more likely than nonleaders to have read specific magazine articles about the campaign and newspaper stories and columns about the election. They were also more likely to have listened to radio speeches and to have followed the political conventions. Furthermore, they were heavy users of the mass media, regardless of their interest in the election—that is, opinion leaders were more likely to use the media than even those nonleaders who were equally interested in the election. Fourth, and most important, there was evidence that the opinion leaders used the ideas and information obtained from the mass media in the advice or information they passed on to their followers:

In the present study we found that one of the functions of opinion leaders is to mediate between the mass media and other people in their groups. It is commonly assumed that individuals obtain their information directly from newspapers, radio, and other media. Our findings, however, did not bear this out. The majority of people acquired much of their information and many of their ideas through personal contacts with the opinion leaders in their groups. These latter individuals, in turn, exposed themselves relatively more than others to the mass media.[8]

This suggestion that information flows from the mass media to the opinion leaders and from them to the mass audience is expressed in the hypothesis of a *two-step flow of communication*. We shall return to this process later.

Case 2 □ Patterns of Influence in a Small Town

Further study of community influentials was conducted by Robert K. Merton, whose research focused on interpersonal influence and communications behavior in a small Eastern community of about 11,000 persons.[9] To locate the influentials, Merton asked his informants to name people to whom they turned for advice or help when making personal decisions (selec-

---

[8] Ibid., p. xxiii.

[9] Robert K. Merton, "Patterns of Influence," in Lazarsfeld and Stanton, *Personal Influence*, pp. 180–219. The findings summarized in this section are selected from several parts of the original work.

tion of furniture, educational plans, choice of a job) and to name persons who, so far as they knew, were generally asked for advice on these matters. Several hundred names were reported, several dozen of which were found to have been mentioned four or more times by the informants; these people constituted the opinion leaders or influentials for purposes of the study. Further information was then gathered from the original respondents and from direct interviews with more than half of the leaders, concerning their communications behavior, the situation in which they exerted influence, and so on. The study design, gathering a wealth of information from a small number of key persons, suggested that this research was exploratory, aimed at the discovery of important hypotheses about interpersonal influence in a community. The researchers hoped initially that their data would help to identify the types of people regarded as influential by their neighbors, to gain clues to the methods through which they became influential, and to determine how their patterns of communications behavior are related to their role as influentials.

In the course of interviewing the townspeople and some of the influentials, Merton and his colleagues made an important discovery that has extended our knowledge about opinion leaders in general and about the link between them and mass communications in particular. It became evident that the entire concept of "the influential" is not adequately specific, for there was no such single type who stood apart from others in the community. Rather, there seemed to be different types of influentials, at least two of which types were evident among the town's opinion leaders. Merton identified these as *local* and *cosmopolitan* influentials. The chief criterion for separating the two types was their orientation toward their town, the local influential being preoccupied essentially with community affairs, the cosmopolitan influential being also concerned with the larger world, both national and international, and its problems.

Once this distinction was made, a considerable part of the research centered on detecting similarities and differences between these two types of influentials. For example, the localite was more likely to have been born in or near the community, whereas the cosmopolitan had been more mobile and was a relative newcomer to the town. Local influentials were also more concerned with knowing a large number of townspeople, whereas cosmopolitans were more restrictive in their associations, tending to make friends with people on the same status level. And local influentials were more likely to participate in voluntary associations designed for making contacts and friends, whereas the cosmopolitan tended to belong to organizations which focused on special skills or interests, such as hobby groups and professional societies.

Local and cosmopolitan influentials also differed markedly in their communications behavior. Both types, to be sure, used the mass media more than did the average person in the community. Nevertheless, they differed in their communications tastes and in the uses to which they put the communications material. Consider, for example, their patterns of magazine reading. Both types of influential read magazines more than the average citizen did. But the cosmopolitan leader was a heavier user, especially of news magazines. Merton explains this difference in terms of the functions magazines serve for each type of influential. For cosmopolites, magazines in general, and news magazines in particular, are an important link with the outside world, providing information that helps to reduce their sense of cultural isolation and enables them to maintain their leadership on nonlocal topics. For localites, on the other hand, news magazines are luxuries, since they do not contain much material about local affairs—the topics upon which they may be called for an opinion. Similarly, although localites read more newspapers, they were local ones, whereas cosmopolites were more likely to be regular readers of the metropolitan New York papers. In the medium of radio, the localites' interest in radio news was limited primarily to straight newscasts, whereas the cosmopolites preferred news commentators and analysts who could help them to interpret events.

Particularly relevant among the many illuminating points about influentials brought out in this study was the discovery that if there were at least two major types of influentials in the community, there might be more. Merton speculates about this possibility and advances the hypothesis that local influentials seem to be *polymorphic*. That is, their connections in town (upon which rests their influence) cover several different fields, and they can exert influence in a variety of spheres of life. On the other hand, Merton suggests, the cosmopolitans' influence is more likely to be *monomorphic*; that is, it is restricted to the field in which they are consulted as an expert—national or international politics, fashions, world business, or some other subject. The following study supports Merton's hypothesis that opinion leadership in such matters tends to fall into several hands.

Case 3 □ Personal Influence in a Larger City

In the spring of 1945 a panel study of opinion leadership was conducted among a random sample of 800 women in Decatur, Illinois, a city of about 60,000 people. The results of this investigation were published in 1955 in *Personal Influence*, by Elihu Katz and Paul Lazarsfeld.[10]

Four problems occupied the researchers throughout this study. First, they were interested in determining the impact of personal influence, as compared with the impact of the mass media, in four areas of common decision-making: marketing, fashions, public issues, and (what was then still common) choice of motion pictures. Second, they investigated characteristics that differentiated opinion leaders from nonleaders in these four areas, especially in terms of the leader's position in the life cycle (for example, young woman or matron), socioeconomic status, and patterns of gregariousness. Third, the researchers investigated the flow of influence—for example, whether it went from the older women to the younger or from the rich to the poor. Fourth, they studied the ways in which personal influence was tied to the mass media, that is, what the communications habits of opinion leaders were and how much these leaders, in turn, were influenced by the mass media. Only the first and last areas of investigation concern us here.

Let us consider first the relative impact of personal *versus* mass communications. In order to study impact, the researchers decided to analyze the role played by the several media in effecting recent changes in opinions or behavior among the members of their sample. For example, women were asked whether they had changed their hair style or their way of dress recently; if they had, they were then asked a series of questions designed

---

[10] Specific page references will be cited only for direct quotations from the study.

to detect the impact of mass and personal communications upon this decision.

How can one determine whether one medium has a greater impact than another upon a person's decision? The concept of impact is a complicated one. For example, does the fact that one medium reaches a larger audience than another mean that it has greater impact? Not necessarily; for the communication that reaches the smaller audience may be more influential in affecting decisions than the communication with the greater coverage. At least two factors are at work here: *coverage* and *persuasiveness*. Coverage can be measured in a variety of standardized ways. But impact cannot; so a new measure had to be invented. The new measure consisted of a simple *index of effectiveness*, which took into account both the amount of exposure achieved by the several media and the relative role each played in the decision itself.

The numerical value of the index of effectiveness is the proportion of persons who assess a particular medium as being most influential in their decision making on some subject to the total number of people making that decision who report being exposed to that medium. In a simple equation:

$$\text{Index of Effectiveness} = \frac{\text{Effective Exposure}}{\text{Total Exposure}}$$

In three of the four areas of decision making under study (marketing, fashions, and motion picture selection) personal contacts had greater influence upon the decision makers than any of the mass media studied, as measured by their index of effectiveness. For example, in marketing decisions, contacts with friends, relatives, or neighbors had an index of effectiveness of .39, in contrast with an index of .25 for radio advertising, .07 for newspaper advertising, and .07 for magazine advertising. These figures do not mean that the mass communications had almost no effect; on the contrary, sometimes the mass media played an important contributory role in the decision making and occasionally they played the decisive role. But the data do underscore the relatively greater impact that face-to-face communications have upon decision makers.

Why should personal communication be a more effective means of persuasion than mass communication? In their earlier study of voting behavior Lazarsfeld and his colleagues suggested five advantageous characteristics of personal relationships.[11] First, personal contacts are more casual, apparently less purposive, and more difficult to avoid than mass communications. Many people are highly selective of mass communications, avoiding materials that go against their personal opinions or in which they are not interested. But people are less likely to anticipate the content of the personal communication or to take steps to avoid it. Second, face-to-face communication permits greater flexibility in content. If the communicator meets resistance from the audience, he or she can change the line of argument to meet audience reactions. Third, the direct personal relationships involved in face-to-face communication can enhance the rewards for accepting the message or argument and the "punishment" for not accepting it. Fourth, some people are more likely to put their trust in the judgment and viewpoint of persons whom they know and respect than in those of the impersonal mass communicator. Fifth, by personal contact the communicator can sometimes achieve his or her purpose without actually persuading the audience to accept a new point of view. In voting, for example, a forceful party worker or a friend may persuade individuals to go to the polls and vote without actually altering or activating their interest in the campaign or their position on the issues.

In the Decatur study, Katz and Lazarsfeld emphasize the advantage of the interpersonal aspects of face-to-face communication in affecting marketing, fashions, and movie selection. The mass media depend primarily on the *content* of their communications, especially on whether the content makes the object or viewpoint presented attractive to the audience. Personal communicaions, on the other hand, influence people not only through what is said but also by personal *control,* in which the source of the directive is as important as the content itself. "People can induce each other," write Katz and Lazarsfeld, "to a variety of activities as a result of their interpersonal relations and thus their influence goes far beyond the content of their communication."[12]

---

[11] Lazarsfeld, Berelson, and Gaudet, *The People's Choice.*

[12] Katz and Lazarsfeld, *Personal Influence,* p. 185. The quotations from this work are by permission of the publisher, Macmillan Publishing Co., Inc.; Copyright 1955 by The Free Press, a Corporation.

Let us now consider a few of the findings about opinion leaders, their communications behavior, and data bearing on the hypothesis of a two-step flow of communications. Opinion leaders were identified in the Decatur study, as in the earlier *The People's Choice*, through their answers to questions about their role in giving advice. For example, each woman was asked both in June and in August, "Have you recently been asked for advice about what pictures to see?" If she said yes, detailed data were gathered about the incidents. Also, each woman was asked in August whether she thought she was more or less likely than other women in her circle of friends to be asked her advice on such topics. From the answers to these questions an index was constructed that separated opinion leaders from nonleaders in each area of opinion under study.

Examination of the characteristics of these opinion leaders gave strong support to many of the hypotheses suggested by the earlier studies on personal influence by Lazarsfeld, Merton, and others. As in *The People's Choice*, where opinion leaders on politics were found in all walks of life, in the Decatur study, opinion leaders on marketing, fashion, public issues, and motion pictures were widely distributed. Each stratum of society seemed to have its own group of opinion leaders. Furthermore, each sphere of life usually had different people serving as opinion leaders, much as there were separate influentials for local and cosmopolitan issues in Merton's study. There was no evidence of a generalized leadership factor that might make an opinion leader in one area more likely to be a leader in others. Considering three areas (fashions, marketing, and public affairs), the researchers found that only 3 percent of the women in the study were opinion leaders in all three fields at the same time; 10 percent were leaders in two fields; 27 percent were opinion leaders in a single area. Hence, at least in areas that do not restrict themselves to local issues, personal influence appears to be monomorphic, as had been suggested in Merton's research on cosmopolitan leaders.[13]

_____

[13] For an alternative view, see Alan Marcus and Raymond Bauer, "Yes: There are Generalized Opinion Leaders," *Public Opinion Quarterly* 28 (1964): 628–632.

What were the communications habits of opinion leaders? Here, too, several of the relationships noted in earlier studies were corroborated. The opinion leaders' generally high exposure to mass media was again documented. First, leaders in every sphere of influence tended to be more highly exposed to mass communications than were the nonleaders. They read more books and magazines than nonleaders and attended the movies more often. Second, the selective nature of exposure to the mass media was again evident. Leaders read magazines that dealt with their specialty, fashion leaders being more likely to read fashion magazines than either nonleaders or opinion leaders in other fields. Opinion leaders in the fields of fashion and public affairs more frequently read mass media that reflect a cosmopolitan orientation (such as out-of-town newspapers and national news magazines) than did leaders in marketing or motion pictures. This gave support to Merton's observation that such media are selected because they serve a specific function for the opinion leader. Third, some support for the two-step flow of communications was obtained:

So far we have seen that the opinion leaders tend to be both more generally exposed to the mass media, and more specifically exposed to the content most closely associated with their leadership. Presumably this increased exposure then becomes a component—witting or unwitting—of the influence which such influentials transmit to others. As a result of these findings, the idea of the "two-step flow of communication" gains credence.[14]

Of course, the term "two-step flow" is more heuristic than definitive; that is, it suggests that some, but by no means all, communication content reaches a mass audience indirectly through the mediating efforts of opinion leaders.[15] But it is quite possible, as, indeed, some of the findings in the Decatur and in subsequent studies would indicate, that there are more than two steps in this process. Sometimes opinion leaders on some topic

---

[14] Katz and Lazarsfeld, *Personal Influence*, p. 316.

[15] Evidence that messages often reach individuals directly without the mediating efforts of opinion leaders is presented, for example, in a voting study by Bernard Berelson, Paul Lazarsfeld, and William McPhee, *Voting* (Chicago: University of Chicago Press, 1954).

look, in turn, to other people for information and advice on that subject. Some of these second-level influentials may depend on the mass media, whereas others turn to still a third circle of opinion leaders for advice, and so on.

That the communication process may be more complex than originally suggested by the term "two-step flow" does not detract from the important reconceptualization signified by the term. The concepts introduced and explored in the three pioneer studies summarized above, and in other related research, have had great impact upon subsequent theoretical and empirical work on the relation between interpersonal and mass communication within the United States and in other societies. Studies have examined the parts played by interpersonal and mass communication in such diverse processes as the adoption and diffusion of innovations, the diffusion of information and news, political elections, consumer behavior, public health campaigns, modernization and other forms of social change, birth control, and a variety of other social phenomena.[16] The scope of these studies has ranged from small communities through selected segments of the population (for example, physicians, scientists, farmers) to larger sectors of the total society.

These new studies have contributed much to our knowledge of the communication process. Nevertheless, a theoretical synthesis of their findings remains premature, because the studies vary in their conceptual definitions, operational measures, and methodologies. Thus it is difficult to tell whether findings from one study genuinely corroborate or contradict those from another. Rather than attempt a comprehensive review of these findings (a task far exceeding the scope of this chapter), we shall select a few recent studies or areas of research that sample, but by no means exhaust, our growing sociological insights into the relation between personal influence and mass communication.

---

[16] The literature on these studies is far too extensive to permit a bibliographic review here. Recent examples can be found in Walter Weiss, "Effects of the Mass Media of Communications," in *The Handbook of Social Psychology*, 2d ed., ed. Gardner Lindzey and Elliot Aronson (Reading, Mass.: Addison-Wesley, 1969), Vol. 5, Ch. 38, and in Everett Rogers, "Mass Media and Interpersonal Communication," in Ithiel de Sola Pool et al., eds., *Handbook of Communication* (Chicago: Rand McNally, 1973), Ch. 11.

Case 4 □ Opinion Seeking, Opinion Avoiding, and
Opinion Leadership

From a sociological perspective opinion leadership is not an
attribute of an individual, like a personality trait, but a social
act or set of acts involving interaction between two or more
individuals. Sociological interest focuses on such questions as the
conditions under which such interaction is likely to occur, the
nature of the interaction, regularities in the social characteristics
of people likely to play the role of opinion leader on various
topics under different conditions, and the communications behavior and other activities of individuals playing the role of
opinion leader or "follower" on some topic. Attention has been
drawn recently to the active role of some "followers" in solicit-
ing opinions, information, or advice from others. This author
and Muriel Cantor, for example, in a study of opinion leadership
and communication behavior among graduate students, demonstrated the value of distinguishing between opinion leadership,
opinion seeking, and opinion avoiding on particular topics. With
regard to one of the topics under study, United States foreign
affairs, it was found that certain individuals actively sought the
opinions of others, whereas some individuals avoided them; persons engaging in either type of activity also might or might not
play the role of opinion leader for others.

They found that:

. . . opinion seekers differ from avoiders in their level of interest
in the topic and related subjects (but not on other matters) and in
exposure to mass media most likely to be relevant to the topic (but
not in exposure to other media) . . . [O]pinion seekers are active
participants in the communications system; they not only seek the
views of their peers but also make relatively greater use of other
media of communication. Many opinion seekers, in turn, serve as
opinion leaders for others. By contrast, the opinion avoiders are relatively isolated from the flow of communication on a particular topic.
Not only do they avoid seeking the views of their peers, but they make
relatively little use of other sources of information about the subject.
They are, in turn, less likely than the opinion seekers to serve as
opinion leaders for others.

The findings further suggest that:

The heavy communications exposure attributed to opinion leaders by
previous studies is correct but reflects the general characteristics of

opinion seeking which many opinion leaders show. Other individuals who do not serve as opinion leaders also display these characteristics if they are opinion seekers. Those opinion leaders who somehow fail to seek the views of their peers are also less likely to be "tuned in" to other sources of communication about their topic.[17]

The authors conclude that opinion seeking should be regarded as a key role in the flow of personal influence and communication.

Wright and Cantor's research was conducted on a limited population and therefore must be interpreted as suggestive rather than as generalizable to the larger society. Nevertheless, the findings illustrate the need to consider a variety of communication roles for the analysis of interpersonal communications and their connection with the mass media.[18]

Case 5 □ International Study of Opinion Makers

Recent research at Columbia University's Bureau of Applied Social Research has extended the tradition of opinion leadership research, which was initiated in the studies of the 1940s, into a new consideration of national elites and the power structure. Comparative studies are underway in the United States, in Yugoslavia, and in several other European nations. The researchers have concentrated on individuals who, primarily because of the formal positions that they hold but not entirely limited to this base, are influential in matters of national concern. The direct link to earlier research on opinion leaders is especially evident in the Bureau's American Leadership project, which follows the tradition of voting studies and research on the phenomenon of local opinion leaders. Allen Barton, a sociologist who is one of the codirectors of this project, places the research within this tradition as follows:

These opinion-leaders tended to read more and listen more to political communications. Therefore the journalists and editors of the mass

---

[17] These extracts from "The Opinion Seeker and Avoider: Steps Beyond the Opinion Leader Concept," by Charles R. Wright and Muriel Cantor, are reprinted from *Pacific Sociological Review* 10 (Spring 1967), pp. 42–43, by permission of the publisher, Sage Publications, Inc.

[18] For a study of the communication linkage role that members of certain occupations play for their clientele in an urban setting, see Judith Beinstein, *Conversations in Semi-public Places* (Ph.D. diss., University of Pennsylvania, 1972).

media and the politicians and interest-group spokesmen whose statements appeared in these media could be considered as remote "opinion-makers" for local opinion-leaders who in turn influenced others. This naturally led to the question, who influenced the "opinion-makers"? Could the method of studying opinion leadership developed in studies of the general public be applied to the national figures who communicate to them through the mass media? Are these leaders of national institutions, the political parties, the economy, and the mass media themselves, interconnected in networks of informal relationships which influence their opinions, norms, ideologies, political behavior, and the content which they communicate to the public?[19]

To answer these and other questions, the researchers selected six major institutional sectors of American society—mass organizations, legislators, government administration, economic administration, mass communication, and intellectuals—and sampled from among individuals who held top formal positions in each sector. These formal leaders were interviewed to determine the extent to which they communicated with the public and one another, proposed public policy, or attempted to influence policy decisions. They also were asked sociometric questions about whom they regarded as generally influential, whom their personal opinion leaders were, and whom their discussion partners on policy questions were. By following the sociometric chain further, it was possible also to locate the opinion leaders and discussion partners of these newly identified "leaders" of the original sample of top national institutional leaders. "By these procedures," the researchers note, "we can locate those who actually function as opinion-makers, within the set of positional leaders of major social institutions and outside that set."

These research projects have clearly demonstrated both the feasibility and the value of the approach. Reports on the early findings are wide ranging, including information about the limits of consensus on economic and foreign policy issues among

[19] Allen H. Barton, "Determinants of Leadership Attitudes in a Socialist Society," Paper of the International Study of Opinion Makers; prepared for the International Political Science Association, Munich, Germany; mimeographed (New York: Bureau of Applied Social Research, 1970). Quotations are from pp. 1–2 and 3, by permission of the author. See also Allen H. Barton, Bogdan Denitch, and Charles Kadushin, eds., *Opinion-Making Elites in Yugoslavia* (New York: Praeger, 1973).

American leaders, the shape of the national power structure, determinants of leadership attitudes, informal social structure of elites, the social circles of intellectuals in the society, communications intake and output among opinion makers in the society, and other matters. Although space does not permit a summary here, one set of findings on the flow of communications among national figures warrants noting; it concerns the relations between elite American intellectuals and "men of power."

This particular line of research stems from the earlier work of Charles Kadushin, a sociologist interested in the study of social circles, a concept related to patterns of personal influence. For purposes of the study, elite intellectuals were considered to be individuals who contributed fairly frequently to magazines or journals that were influential among intellectuals or individuals who were designated as influential intellectuals by these writers. Men of power were identified by their positions in various institutional sectors, as described above. Kadushin examined the extent to which intellectuals were nominated as influentials by men in positions of power and the extent to which intellectuals reported that they had direct contact with such national decision makers. Little direct interpersonal communication occurred. Relatively few American intellectuals directly communicated with men of power on social and political matters; and men of power rarely sought the views of intellectuals, except on matters requiring technical expertise. Nevertheless, Kadushin points out, intellectuals may have an indirect influence on men of power through a "trickle down" process of communication.

It was found that various leaders in the mass media and men of power in other sectors of the elite either occasionally or frequently read the magazines and journals of opinion in which intellectuals publish—the *New York Times Magazine*, *Foreign Affairs*, *Harper's*, and the *Atlantic*, to mention but a few. These media of communication provide one important channel through which a society's intellectuals can have an indirect effect on men of power and, through them, on social policy. In addition, it is possible that through their writings and other public activities intellectuals helped create a general climate of opinion within which social problems were defined and policies formed. Nevertheless, Kadushin notes, by and large the writings and other public communications of intellectuals were directed more at one another than at the power elite.[20]

The discussion of research on the connections between personal influence and mass communication among selected segments of the population such as the power elites may appear to the reader to be somewhat afield from our concern with the mass audience. Nonetheless, these studies reflect persistent and theoretically important sociological interest in analysis of interpersonal and mass communication behavior as related to the study of social structure, social order, and social change. We turn now to another example of such concern, exemplified chiefly through the work of rural sociologists interested in the role of communication in the adoption of innovations and their diffusion within a community.

Case 6 ☐ Adoption and Diffusion of Innovations

For many years sociologists have been interested in studying the adoption of a variety of innovations in farming, health practices, consumer behavior, family-planning practices, and other areas of life. For example, as early as the 1920s, but mainly since the 1940s, rural sociologists have been studying the problem of how technological innovations were learned about and adopted by farmers. Insofar as the adoption of innovations (in farming or in other areas) requires voluntary acceptance by individuals, it may share some features of individual decision making on other matters, such as voting.

Investigations of the adoption process have considered, among other things, the relative roles played by mass communication and by interpersonal communication in the acceptance or rejection of innovations. A second thrust of these investigations concerns the diffusion of the innovation within the community—that is, the rate of acceptance of an innovation by the various individuals for whom it is relevant. These studies also consider the

---

[20] Charles Kadushin, Herman Kane, and Stella Manne, "The Relations between Elite American Intellectuals and Men of Power" (Paper presented at the annual meeting of the American Sociological Association, 1973, mimeographed.) See also Carol Weiss, "What America's Leaders Read," *Public Opinion Quarterly* 38 (Spring 1974): 1–22; and Charles Kadushin, *The American Intellectual Elite* (Boston: Little, Brown, 1974).

roles played by mass communication and interpersonal communication in diffusion. It is not possible to summarize here more than fifty years of domestic and international research on adoption and diffusion, but fortunately, several summaries are available elsewhere.[21] In this section we shall simply note two important ways in which this line of research has forced or reinforced some refinements in the conceptualization of the problem. Stated most simply, the two ways have emphasized that adoption should be examined as a process rather than as an event and that diffusion should be analyzed as a social process rather than as simply the sum of individual adoptions.

To the observer, and perhaps to the individual involved, adoption of an innovation may seem to be an event or act: the farmer plants a new type of seed or does not; a consumer buys a colored television set or does not; a woman accepts some new device for preventing pregnancy or does not. In similar fashion, many other kinds of decisions by the individual may seem to be events: a citizen votes or does not, votes for one candidate or another, chooses a movie to see, buys a new automobile, or gets married. In each instance there is an apparent salient moment at which an act takes place that signifies the decision: one votes, buys, uses, or otherwise engages in some behavior different from the past. But upon reflection it can be seen that this apparently final act is really only a part of a longer process of thought and activity that precedes it, accompanies it, and may follow it. To conceptualize the adoption of an innovation or any other kind of individual decision making as part of a process rather than as an isolated random act without a history is an important step, albeit "self-evident" once expressed. This conceptualization was one of the underlying reasons behind the use of the panel technique by Lazarsfeld and his associates in their early studies of "votes in the making." What has been emphasized by the work of students of adoption is the need to systematically specify and codify apparent steps or "stages" in

[21] See, as examples, Everett M. Rogers and Floyd Shoemaker, *Communication of Innovations* (New York: Free Press, 1971); Everett Rogers, *Modernization Among Peasants* (New York: Holt, Rinehart & Winston, 1969); Elihu Katz, Martin Levin, and Herbert Hamilton, "Traditions of Research on the Diffusion of Innovation," *American Sociological Review* 28 (April 1963): 237–252.

the individual's decision to adopt or to reject an innovation, or in any other decision for that matter.

Varying numbers of such stages have been postulated by different students of the problem. A model that has been commonly advanced for many years consists of five stages: awareness, interest, evaluation, trial, and adoption or rejection. The model suggests that in order for an individual to adopt an innovation, he or she must first become aware of its existence, become interested in knowing more about it, evaluate its relevance to personal needs, decide to give it a small trial, then assess the experiences with the trial and decide to adopt or reject the innovation. Other models have reduced the number of apparent stages; some have added postadoption decisions to continue or to discontinue the new activity. In some cases it is argued that the stages need not follow the order of the model; some might even be by-passed under certain circumstances. Many other modifications appear in the literature.

One important result of this line of investigation has been to focus attention on the possibility that various media of communication, both mass and interpersonal, play differentially important roles for the individual at different stages in the decision to adopt or reject an innovation. Some findings suggest that the mass media sometimes serve better than interpersonal communications as sources of first awareness of the existence of a new idea, new technique, or other innovation. And some studies suggest that interpersonal communications and personal influence play a more important role than the mass media in later stages in the process. Despite the many available studies of the relationship between communication and adoption, the findings do not permit a firm set of conclusions. Much needs to be done by way of investigating the sociological *conditions* under which the various modes of communication contribute to the adoption phenomenon. But these studies have supported a theoretical perspective of interpersonal and mass communication as related, perhaps as complementary, modes rather than as unrelated fully self-sufficient systems of communication.

The second major conceptual contribution of research on adoption comes from its consideration of diffusion as a social process. The process of diffusion of an innovation or idea within a community can be segmented into stages for purposes of analysis. Individuals are classified according to whether they adopt the innovation relatively early or late in its diffusion. Some authors contend that diffusion often follows a distribution resembling a normal curve. But regardless of whether or not one accepts this model, it is possible to classify individuals as relatively early or late adopters if one can secure information on the time at which they adopted the new practice. One scheme classifies individuals as innovators, early adopters, early majority, late majority, and laggards. Researchers have examined the roles played by mass communications and by interpersonal communications for individuals thus classified by time of their adoption of the innovation. Some studies suggest that mass media are more salient for relatively early adopters and that interpersonal communications play a more important role for later adopters. The picture is complex and in need of much more systematic research. The role of opinion leaders in the diffusion process also has been examined, and distinctions have been made between the role of innovator and of opinion leader. The uses of various sources of communication by persons playing these and other roles in the diffusion process have been examined, but much more work needs to be done before our sociological picture of the process is clear.

We turn now to our final example of an area of research relating personal and mass communications—the study of the diffusion of news.

Case 7 □ How News Gets Around

Research on how people learn of important or routine news events has contributed to our knowledge on such points as which media provide initial and supplementary information, how long it takes for the news to flow to various segments of the population, and what part personal contacts play in this communications process. An early example of such research is a study made in 1953 by two sociologists, Otto Larsen and Richard J. Hill, of the diffusion of news about the death of United States Senator Robert A. Taft, an event that occurred across the continent from Seattle, the site of the research.[22]

Senator Taft died in New York City on a Friday morning, at

---

[22] Otto Larsen and Richard J. Hill, "Mass Media and Interpersonal Communication in the Diffusion of a News Event," *American Sociological Review* 19 (August 1954): 426–443.

7:30 A.M. Seattle time; wire service accounts of his death reached there by 7:45 A.M. Within fifteen minutes Seattle's six major radio stations had broadcast the news; the story was on television at 10:45 A.M. (the first telecast of the day); and it was available in the newspapers downtown at 2:30 P.M (several hours later than would be normal for Seattle because of a newspaper strike). On Saturday the researchers interviewed approximately 150 men and women living in a housing project for faculty members of the University of Washington. On Monday evening they held nearly 150 interviews with residents of an interracial working-class housing project near the industrial section of Seattle. These two sets of interviews provided the basic data for the study.

The news was diffused widely and quickly. By the time of the interviews fully 88 percent of the faculty community and 93 percent of the community of laborers knew of Senator Taft's death. The highest proportion of persons reported first hearing about the death on the radio. But, outside of this, the patterns of obtaining the news differed greatly between the two communities. Among the faculty group, the second highest proportion cited interpersonal communication as their first source of the news, and relatively few first learned of the event from television or the newspaper. This pattern held for both men and women. Among the workers, on the other hand, television was the second most important source of news of the event, and newspapers and interpersonal communications nearly tied for third and fourth places. Here, however, the communications habits of men and women differed. By and large, the working-class women first heard of Senator Taft's death by radio and television; eight out of every ten women reported this, as compared with only five out of every ten men. Working-class men were more likely than working-class women to have obtained the news from newspapers and word-of-mouth communication. Once they had heard the news, about six out of every ten faculty members and three out of ten workers searched around for more information about the event. The faculty group used radio as the immediate source of supplementary information, and the laboring group turned to the newspaper.

What light does the study shed on the connection between personal and mass communications? The study has several broad implications. First, it emphasizes the importance of primary groups in personal communication about events. Those who first heard the news by word of mouth usually got it from another family member or from a coworker. Second, there is strong evidence that people do more than just listen to mass-communicated news—they talk about it with friends, relatives, neighbors, and coworkers. At least 80 percent of the people who learned about the senator's death discussed it with others, each person talking with approximately three others. Not all these conversations resulted in spreading the news to those who had not already heard it; in fact, only about 15 percent of the reported conversations did so. Nevertheless, of those who first heard about the event from one of the mass media, from 12 to 29 percent passed this news on to another person, in addition to holding noninformative conversations about the topic with others. Hence the study provides additional support for the two-step flow hypothesis.

Another example of the rapid local diffusion of news about a tragic event is provided by a study made in Dallas, Texas, shortly following the assassination of President John F. Kennedy there in November 1963.[23] Interviews were conducted with a modified area probability sample of approximately 200 Dallas residents. News that the President had been shot reached two-thirds of the sample within fifteen minutes of the event, and within two hours 95 percent of the respondents had learned of the assassination (all knew by 6:00 P.M., five and a half hours after the shooting). The majority of respondents first heard the news from interpersonal communications, face to face or through telephone calls; the rest were informed by television or radio. And the news spread almost as rapidly by word of mouth as it did by the mass media, reaching most people within an hour of the first news release. It is likely, of course, that the initial source of the news for some of the individuals who then passed it along to others was a television or radio news bulletin. Therefore, the role of the mass media was magnified through diffusion by interpersonal communications, again demonstrating the importance of the multistep flow of communication.

---

[23] Charles M. Bonjean, Richard J. Hill, and Harry W. Martin, "Reactions to the Assassination in Dallas," in *The Kennedy Assassination and the American Public*, ed. Bradley Greenberg and Edwin Parker (Stanford, Calif.: Stanford University Press, 1965), pp. 178–198.

The complementary role of interpersonal and mass communications in diffusion of news of the assassination was not limited to Dallas. A nationwide survey by the National Opinion Research Corporation (NORC), conducted within days following the assassination, provides similar data.[24] About two-thirds of the nation's adults heard the news about the assassination within thirty minutes of the shooting; in less than two hours 92 percent knew about it; and by 6:00 P.M. 99.8 percent had heard about it. The news first reached about half the people by radio or television and the other half by telephone calls or other personal communications. (The researchers note that an NORC survey conducted in 1945 showed that news of President Franklin D. Roosevelt's death reached about half the public through mass communications and the other half through personal communications.) After receiving the news, many people, as might be expected, turned to the mass media for further details and to other people for discussion of the tragedy.

Studies have been made of the diffusion of other items of news, some stories of less importance than the death of a President or a senator, others of similarly high news value. Among the items studied were the admission of Alaska to statehood, the launching of America's first satellite, President Eisenhower's stroke, Eisenhower's decision to seek a second term as President, the results of a heavyweight boxing match, the issuing of a Papal Encyclical on birth control, and the shooting of Governor Wallace of Alabama.[25] It has been suggested by communication

---

[24] Paul B. Sheatsley and Jacob J. Feldman, "A National Survey of Public Reactions and Behavior," in Greenberg and Parker, *The Kennedy Assassination and the American Public*, pp. 149–177.

[25] For examples, see Greenberg and Parker, *The Kennedy Assassination and the American Public.* See also Delbert C. Miller, "A Research Note on Mass Communications," *American Sociological Review* 10 (1945): 691–694; Paul Deutschmann and Wayne Danielson, "Diffusion of Knowledge of the Major News Story," *Journalism Quarterly* 37 (1960): 345–355; Wayne Danielson, "Eisenhower's February Decision," *Journalism Quarterly* 33 (1956): 433–441; Bradley Greenberg, "Person-to-Person Communication in the Diffusion of News Events," *Journalism Quarterly* 41 (1964): 489–494; Bradley Greenberg, James Brinton, and Richard Farr, "Diffusion of News About an Anticipated Major News Event," *Journal of Broadcasting* 9 (1965): 129–142; John Adams, James Mullen, and Harold Wilson, "Diffusion of a 'Minor' Foreign Affairs News Event," *Journalism Quarterly* 46 (1969): 545–551; and David Schwartz, "How Fast Does News Travel," *Public Opinion Quarterly* 37 (1973–1974): 625–627.

researcher Bradley Greenberg, as well as by Wilbur Schramm and others, that there is a curvilinear relation between the news value of a story and the speed and channels by which it reaches the public.[26] Stories of little news value (or that have been suppressed by the mass media) are likely to be diffused through word of mouth, as is news about major events. More routine news items, covered by the mass media, are likely to reach most people first through the mass media communications, although some people still will learn of these events from others. The time of day when the event occurs also affects its pattern of distribution. Other factors include where people are and what they are doing when a story breaks.

It would be misleading, however, to interpret these findings as evidence of mass media *versus* personal communication. Both kinds of communication play a role in the news diffusion process, especially as this process expands to include activities following first awareness of an event, when individuals often seek additional information, interpretation, and evaluation from the mass media and from discussions among themselves.

If we appear to have belabored the relationship between mass communication and personal communication, the stress is deliberate. It is all too easy to think of the audience for any of the mass media as having only this medium of exposure in common and as having it as an isolated communication experience. Our sociological perspective stresses the need to examine exposure to mass communication within the social context surrounding the individual, including his or her experiences with other mass media and interpersonal communications with family members, friends, coworkers, and others who, too, make up the "mass audience."

OTHER ASPECTS OF THE MASS AUDIENCE

During the past several decades considerable research has been conducted in the field of audience analysis. This research includes studies of the demographic and other social characteristics of audiences for certain media, overlap among the media's audiences, the nature of fans and abstainers, the uses

---

[26] See Wilbur Schramm, "Communication in Crisis," in Greenberg and Parker, *The Kennedy Assassination and the American Public*, pp. 1–25.

to which individuals put the media and the gratifications derived thereby, and the selective communications behavior of people of similar or different social backgrounds.

Much data have been gathered on the demographic characteristics of mass media audiences. Sometimes these studies provide a statistical profile of the audience: the proportions of men and women, age composition, educational distribution, income levels, occupational categories, and the like. At other times studies provide data on the mass media exposure of individuals from various social categories, for example, as to what proportion of men or women read a daily newspaper. These descriptive statistics have sociological interest, since, as Robert K. Merton has noted, "such categories as sex, age, education and income happen also to correspond to some of the chief statuses in the social structure."[27] Findings for various media audiences are too numerous and diverse to permit summary here. By and large the audiences for various mass media differ more significantly in their social characteristics than in any recognizable personality traits. For example, the use of print media increases with level of education of the individual, although amount of television viewing does not. And the types of media content consumed, as well as the uses to which the media are put, appear related to social characteristics.

Such empirical generalizations about mass media audiences can be derived from diverse independent sources, including commercial surveys. They provide a useful first step. But fuller sociological analysis requires special efforts to relate communications behavior to social structure, to measure audience changes and trends and their correlates, and to make comparative studies across cultures. A good example of the value of continuity in social research on audiences is sociologist Robert T. Bower's study of the American television audience in 1970, which purposely replicated many of the questions from an earlier (1960) national survey of television behavior and attitudes.[28] Future replications of this and other studies are needed to develop social

---

[27] Robert K. Merton, *Social Theory and Social Structure* (Glencoe, Ill.: Free Press, 1949) p. 212.

[28] Robert T. Bower, *Television and the Public* (New York: Holt, Rinehart & Winston, 1973).

indicators of changes in media audiences and to establish a firmer base for empirical generalizations.

Few members of modern societies are unexposed to mass communication in some form. Examination of the extent of overlap among media audiences and the ways in which such patterns of media exposure relate to other social and social psychological factors is of continuing interest to sociologists. A variety of studies have demonstrated a tendency toward "all-or-none" exposure to mass communications.[29] This phrase does not mean that people either use all of the media or none. Rather, it means that people who are heavy users of one medium are also likely to use others fairly regularly; and people who avoid one medium in particular are also likely to restrict their use of others. Nor does the all-or-none pattern imply that there is no competition for audiences. Indeed, the invasion by television of the leisure-time market has sharply cut into the time audiences formerly spent on radio, movies, and other activities. Nevertheless, certain people tend to be more media-minded than others, and they manage their leisure hours so as to permit some regular use of all the mass media available to them. Attempts have been made to classify individuals according to their patterns of media use—for example, heavy or light use of newspapers, combined with heavy or light use of television—and to examine how such usage correlates with other social characteristics of the individual, such as knowledge about social events and participation in political and social activities. Recent examples can be found in studies by John Robinson and by the writer.[30]

The uses to which individuals put various mass media and the gratification that they receive from these media have been of sociological interest for many decades. Early research on listeners to radio daytime serial programs is an example. Recently

---

[29] See Paul Lazarsfeld and Patricia Kendall, *Radio Listening in America* (New York: Prentice-Hall, 1948), Ch. 1.

[30] John Robinson, "Mass Communication and Information Diffusion," in *Current Perspectives in Mass Communication Research*, ed. F. Gerald Kline and Philip J. Tichenor, Sage Annual Review of Communication Research, Vol. I (Beverly Hills, Calif.: Sage Publications, 1972), Ch. 3. Also see Charles R. Wright, "Social Structure and Mass Communication Behavior: New Directions for Audience Analysis," *The Idea of Social Structure: Papers in Honor of Robert K. Merton*, ed. L. Coser (New York: Harcourt Brace Jovanovich, 1975).

this area of study has received renewed attention, especially through the efforts of such sociologists as Jay Blumler, Denis McQuail, and Elihu Katz.[31] A recent study by Katz, Michael Gurevitch, and Hadassah Haas provides a good example.[32] The researchers asked a cross section of Israeli adults to specify how much each of five mass media—books, movies, newspapers, radio, and television—helped to satisfy each of some thirty-five social and psychological needs that could be expected to be met by the mass media. In addition, each person was asked what else helped to satisfy each need. In this way the researchers were able to identify a variety of uses of mass media and their attendant gratification of needs. Interestingly, interpersonal communications with friends, family, and others often rivaled the mass media as sources of satisfaction of communication needs.

Selective exposure, an especially important pattern of communication behavior, warrants attention before closing this section. Early sociological studies of mass communications in natural field settings indicated a tendency for exposure to mass communications to be biased in favor of individuals who are most interested in the communication content and who hold opinions and views generally in agreement with that content. By contrast, individuals having less interest or contrary views, or both, were less likely to be exposed to the communication. During election campaigns, for example, Democrats and Republicans were more likely to be heavily exposed to their own party's communications than to those of their opponents (although it is by no means the case that all voters were exposed to only the messages from their own party). Such empirically discovered patterns of communications behavior have been recently labeled de facto *selective exposure.*[33]

---

[31] See Jay Blumler and Elihu Katz, eds., *Current Perspectives in Mass Communication Research,* Sage Annual Review, Vol. III (Beverly Hills, Calif.: Sage Publications, forthcoming).

[32] Elihu Katz, Michael Gurevitch, and Hadassah Haas, "On the Uses of the Mass Media for Important Things," *American Sociological Review* 38 (1973): 164–181.

[33] The principle of selective exposure appears to have more acceptance among sociologists than among psychologists. For a discussion of some of the issues involved, see the several papers in Robert Abelson et al., eds., *Theories of Cognitive Consistency: A Sourcebook* (Chicago: Rand McNally, 1968), pp. 769–800. These papers, with some exception, stress a psychological perspective. Also see Wilbur Schramm, "Channels and Audiences," in Pool et al., *Handbook of Communication,* Ch. 5.

It is not clear what combinations of social and possibly psychological factors bring such patterns about. Possibly, selective exposure is a by-product of other social characteristics of audience members, for example, education and social class. It is impossible to determine clearly, on the basis of available research, the extent to which such patterns are the direct product of audience members' actively selecting their communications experiences to fit prior interests, needs, and predispositions.[34] We know that individuals differ in their preferences for communication content and that such differences are related to other social characteristics.[35] For example, programs that seem more serious than light—classical music, discussions of public affairs, and forums, as distinguished from popular music, comedies, and mysteries—are more likely to appeal to older persons and people with more formal education than to younger people and people with less formal education. The relation between "serious" communication tastes and such primary social characteristics as age and educational background cannot be explained simply in terms of the greater reading skills of the more educated, for the preferences also carry over to such "spectator" media as radio and television, in which the audience need only listen or watch.

It is possible that selective exposure implies active selection by potential audience members, that people select the mass media and content that they believe will be most interesting and will favor their initial views, opinions, and experiences. Such practices need not be determined by idiosyncratic psychological traits of individual audience members. To a great extent the interests and predispositions that guide audiences in their self-selection have roots in the group structure within which each audience

---

[34] One recent exploratory study of media use among adults living in a suburb between New York and Philadelphia supports a typology of patterns of communications behavior that is internally consistent for each individual. Certain respondents demonstrated *saturation* exposure, frequently using all available mass media; other were *source selective*, generally following whatever is presented by one medium; others were *topic selective*, seeking out communications about some topic of interest regardless of the medium in which it appeared; and a few were *avoiders*, rarely using any of the mass media. See Linda Shipley, *Communication Behavior of People Living in a Megalopolis: A Study of Mass Media Use and Interpersonal Communications of Commuters and Local Workers* (Ph.D. diss., University of Pennsylvania, 1974).

[35] For recent evidence on television audience preferences and selectivity, see Bower, *Television and the Public.*

member lives. Lazarsfeld's account of selective exposure, proposed more than twenty-five years ago, remains timely today:

> In all the fields that have been touched by communications research the self-selection of audiences plays a considerable role. People with political convictions read the newspapers that correspond to their opinions. People with hobbies read the sections of the newspaper which report on these hobbies most fully. This seemingly trivial observation becomes more interesting as we add to it certain corollary findings which can be gleaned from a variety of studies. It has been found, for instance, that people are inclined to read the same news items in newspapers which they have already heard discussed on the radio. In general, they do not look for information on new topics in magazines but for more information on topics with which they are already acquainted.
>
> . . . In general, then, people look not for new experiences in the mass media but for a repetition and an elaboration of their old experiences into which they can more easily project themselves. If we assume then that the types of experiences they have had are determined more by their social roles and context rather than by their psychological traits, it is not surprising that we find primary characteristics [age, sex, educational classification] so dominant in the correlations which communications research has unearthed.[36]

Thus our analysis of the mass audience returns once more to the persistent role of social variables in accounting for audience behavior. We will do well to keep in mind the importance of these social factors when we examine some effects of mass communication on the individual and society in Chapter 6.

CONCLUDING NOTE ON THE CONCEPT OF AUDIENCE

Throughout this chapter we have followed the convention of referring to the users of mass media and of interpersonal communications as audiences. In a sociological sense this remains problematic. A true sociological conceptualization and analysis of the audience will entail new theories and further research. It requires consideration of the normative and organizational components of audiences per se. What are the folkways, mores, and laws that determine who should be members of a particular

---

[36] Paul Lazarsfeld, "Communication Research and the Social Psychologist." Reprinted from *Current Trends in Social Psychology*, Wayne Dennis, ed., by permission of the University of Pittsburgh Press. © 1948 by the University of Pittsburgh Press, pp. 242–244.

audience, how they should behave while playing the role of audience members, and what their rights and obligations are in relation to others in the audience, to the performers, and to members of the society not in the audience? What is the social structure of assembled audiences? How, if at all, are audiences organized? What is the larger social and cultural context within which an audience occurs? These questions are but a brief sampling of the kinds of problems that need to be examined from a sociological perspective. In the current chapter we have perhaps presented less a sociological analysis of the audience than an account of several sociological aspects of audiences. That, however, is the present state of the discipline.

5

cultural content of american mass communications

Every American is familiar with programs, stories, features, and other materials presented by our mass media. Why, then, should such widely recognized elements of everyday life as comic strips, soap operas, and television shows require scientific research? Isn't our common firsthand knowledge about these subjects sufficient for sociological analysis? Why should we *study* mass media content?

WHY STUDY MASS MEDIA CONTENT?

At least three reasons for the systematic study of content can be offered. First, despite our frequent exposure to mass communications, this personal experience is both limited and selective. For example, it is impossible for any of us to watch all the television programs broadcast even in our own communities during an average day or week. Furthermore, because we are highly selective in our exposure, our knowledge about what is being transmitted is biased by our personal tastes. Hence only a systematic monitoring of all broadcasts would give us a representative view of the range of television output. Second, we tend to overgeneralize from our particular communication experiences. For example, if we happen to witness several television programs that feature violence, we are inclined to assume that most television fare reflects violence. Finally, in our daily exposure to mass communications we are seldom motivated to analyze the sociologically meaningful aspects of the content. In viewing television for our personal entertainment, for instance, we are not ordinarily prompted to note or analyze the social class or occupational characteristics of the heroes, heroines, villains, or villainesses on the screen. Content analysis can provide us with the necessary perspective and accurate and sociologically important data on the products of American mass communication.

Content analysis, for our purposes here, is a research technique for the objective, systematic, and sociologically relevant description of mass communication content. The description and analysis may employ either quantitative or qualitative procedures, or both. Objectivity requires that the categories of analysis be so clearly and operationally defined that other researchers can follow them with a fairly high degree of reliability. For example, analysis of the social-class membership of characters in a comic strip or television serial requires a clear specification of the criteria by which the social-class membership can be identified and classified. Systematic analysis requires that *all* the relevant content be considered in terms of the meaningful categories. Thus systematic analysis is distinguished from critical or analytical reading, viewing, or listening, in which reviewers may select any part of the content that supports their argument. For example, if you believe that television programs portray scientists in an unfavorable light, you probably can find a few television shows in which the scientists appear villainous, dishonest, or generally despicable. At the same time, someone with an opposite opinion can as easily find equally dramatic examples of scientists who are portrayed heroically. Neither viewer would be conducting a content analysis, however, for each has *selected* cases to illustrate his or her point. Obviously what is needed is an unbiased overview of the relative frequency of favorable and unfavorable characterizations of scientists—an overview that can come only from classifying *all* the scientists in a representative sample of television programing.

The uses of content analysis are many and varied. Researchers have used content analysis not only to study the characteristics of communication content, but also to draw inferences about the nature of the communicator, the audience, and effects. Research on content characteristics includes studies of trends, international comparisons, propaganda techniques, style, and so on. Sometimes content is analyzed to provide insights into its producers—their intentions or political or psychological states. Occasionally, content is taken as a clue to the nature of audiences—their values, likes, and dislikes. Finally, content is at times interpreted in terms of its presumed effect upon the audience or society.

It is important to remember, however, that content analysis itself provides no *direct* evidence on the nature of the communicator, audience, or effects. Therefore, great caution must be exercised whenever this technique is used for any purpose other than the straightforward description and analysis of the manifest content of the communication. If, for example, we find that scientists are portrayed unfavorably on television, we cannot use this as evidence that television writers or producers *intend* to portray scientists unfavorably. Nor can we claim that these unfavorable stereotypes will deflect students from scientific careers. Such interpretations of the content in terms of probable motives or effects go beyond the available data. Ideally, to know what motivated the portraits, we would need research on the communicators themselves; to discover the consequences of the stereotypes, we would need direct audience research. In the absence of direct evidence on communicator or effects, however, researchers sometimes prefer to make inferences about them from content analysis rather than to speculate on such matters with no data at all.

A detailed survey of the many subjects that have been investigated through content analysis is beyond the scope of this book. Examples can be found in several works.[1] In the remainder of this chapter we will discuss a few illustrative content analyses bearing on some sociologically interesting topics: the presentation of heroes and villains, work, minorities, and socially approved goals and means.

---

[1] Bernard Berelson, *Content Analysis in Communication Research* (Glencoe, Ill.: The Free Press, 1952); Ithiel de Sola Pool, ed., *Trends in Content Analysis* (Urbana: University of Illinois Press, 1959); Robert North et al., *Content Analysis* (Evanston: Northwestern University Press, 1963); George Gerbner et al., eds., *The Analysis of Communication Content* (New York: Wiley, 1969); Ole Holsti, *Content Analysis for the Social Sciences and Humanities* (Reading, Mass.: Addison-Wesley, 1969).

SOCIETY'S HEROES AND VILLAINS

A frequently cited content analysis providing clues to our cultural heroes is Leo Lowenthal's early study of biographies in popular magazines.[2] We noted earlier that one sign of high status in a mass society is to be singled out for attention by the mass media. Perhaps an even greater sign is to be selected as the subject of a biography in one of the popular media. To some extent biographies are the life histories of cultural heroes or villains, from whose experiences the reader can learn lessons of success or failure. Whether or not the reader actually accepts the characters as role models is, of course, a separate empirical question, unanswerable by content analysis. But knowledge about the kinds of persons selected for biographical attention should aid our understanding of American culture as presented by the mass media.

Lowenthal analyzed a systematic sample of all biographies appearing in two popular magazines—*Collier's* and the *Saturday Evening Post*—for the first four decades of the twentieth century. Certain trends appeared during the forty-year span. The "idols" selected for biographies near the beginning of the span were very different from those at the end. "Idols of production," in the spheres of politics, business, and the professions, dominated the earlier period; "idols of consumption," primarily from the field of entertainment, achieved prominence in the more modern time. Even among the biographies of entertainers Lowenthal noted a shift of attention away from those who might be placed in the classical or "serious" arts (literature, fine arts, dance, classical music, theater) toward heroes and heroines of the popular arts. To illustrate, fully 77 percent of the entertainers written about in the biographies prior to World War I were persons from the "serious" arts; during the 1920s the proportion dropped to 38 percent; and by 1940–1941 less than one in ten biographies of entertainers dealt with the "serious" entertainer.

The qualitative content of these biographies shifted too. Older popular biographies contain a good deal of information on the subject's character development, early history, and behavior that

---

[2] Leo Lowenthal, "Biographies in Popular Magazines," in Paul Lazarsfeld and Frank Stanton, eds., *Radio Research 1942–43* (New York: Duell, Sloan and Pearce, 1943), pp. 507–548.

had led to success. Later biographies tend to gloss over the details of character development and give more attention to private life and leisure-time activities. Often the stories of success in the more recent biographies are told in terms of the hero's inherent character traits combined with a series of hardships and "lucky breaks" along the road to success. Lowenthal argues that such a formula is hardly useful as a model for others. It defines success as largely an accidental and irrational event and reflects a degree of normlessness about patterns for achievement in the world.

Among the many other qualitative (and quantitative) differences between the earlier and more modern biographies documented in the study, one warrants special mention here because it suggests an important function of modern biographies for the average reader. Lowenthal discovered a tendency for the new biographies to stress the consumer habits, likes, and dislikes of the popular heroes. In interpreting this new focus (an interpretation that, of course, must go beyond the data of the content analysis itself), Lowenthal suggests that it provides readers with a frame of reference about success within which they are less likely to suffer by comparison with the "great" persons of our times:

. . . the distance between what an average individual may do and the forces and powers that determine his life and death has become so unbridgeable that identification with normalcy, even with Philistine boredom, becomes a readily grasped empire of refuge and escape. It is some comfort for the little man who has become expelled from the Horatio Alger dream, who despairs of penetrating the thicket of grand strategy in politics and business, to see his heroes as a lot of guys who like or dislike highballs, cigarettes, tomato juice, golf and social gatherings—just like himself. He knows how to converse in the sphere of consumption and here he can make no mistakes. By narrowing his focus of attention he can experience the gratification of being confirmed in his own pleasures and discomforts by the great. The large confusing issues in the political and economic realm and the antagonisms and controversies in the social realm—all of these are submerged in the experience of being at one with the lofty and great in the sphere of consumption.[3]

Theodore Greene, who in 1970 published a content analysis of biographies found in a sample of leading American magazines

---

[3] Ibid., pp. 547–548. By permission of Hawthorn Books, Inc.

from 1787 through 1918, takes exception to Lowenthal's interpretation.[4] Greene differs with Lowenthal's "favorable assess-
ment" of the "idols of production" around 1900 and questions
some of his "despairing conclusions" about the "idols of consumption" in the 1940s. Greene's thesis centers on the demise
of individualism as a basic value in America. He sees the heroes
of popular biographies shifting from important figures in the
traditional basic institutions of society (for example, state,
church, and military) during the early years of the Republic, to
idols of power and individualism (creative artists, captains of
industry, empire builders) around the turn of the century, to
idols of justice (politicians) just prior to World War I, and then
toward idols of organization (nonindividualistic leaders in business, politics, government bureaucracy) from 1914–1918.
Greene's study provides interesting information about such components of the biographies as standards of success and the hero's
social relations, education, occupation, and personal character
and habits. His study adds further historical perspective to the
topic of changing cultural heroes.

Many of the qualitative tendencies noted by Lowenthal in the
biographies in the 1940s may persist today. That they extended
into the latter 1950s is indicated by an unpublished study of
biographies in the *Saturday Evening Post* from July 1956 to June
1957. This content analysis revealed an even greater proportion
of idols coming from the world of entertainment; almost all
these idols came from such popular media as radio, television,
and motion pictures.[5] As in Lowenthal's cases, few clues were
given about character development and patterns of success. And
the emphasis on private lives and habits continued. New comparative studies are needed to determine contemporary tendencies in popular biographies and to address such important
questions as the biographical treatment of women as compared
with men.

Lowenthal's study is a blend of quantitative and qualitative
content analysis in which cultural heroes are explicitly identified
as subjects of popular biographies. Turning to another popular

---

[4] Theodore Greene, *America's Heroes: The Changing Models of Success
in American Magazines* (New York: Oxford University Press, 1970).
[5] Unpublished paper by Kenneth Poole, while a graduate student in the
Department of Sociology, University of California, Los Angeles, 1958.

mass medium, television, provides an illustration of a quantitative content analysis that broadens the concepts of heroes and villains to characters portraying such roles in fiction. Our first example stems from the early days of television in America, and although its findings may be dated, it serves to illustrate a contemporary mode of content analysis. We shall follow it with selections from more recent research.

In 1953 a content analysis was made of all television programs broadcast in New York City during the first week of January.[6] In part of the study, conducted by Dallas Smythe for the National Association of Educational Broadcasters, eighty-six drama programs originally produced for television and telecast during that week were analyzed, first in terms of the settings and the kinds of characters in this television "world," then in terms of the social and psychological characteristics of the heroes, villains, and supporting characters, finally in terms of the qualities attributed to occupational groups in the stories.

Television drama during the week studied mainly portrayed contemporary but fictitous American settings. Men outnumbered women in the casts by a ratio of about 2 to 1. Very young people (under twenty) and very old people (over sixty) were underrepresented in the stories, which focused primarily on persons at the height of the courting and child-bearing ages, who are employed or employable. Such white-collar positions as managers and professionals with higher statuses were heavily overrepresented at the expense of the routine white-collar and blue-collar jobs. Service workers and household workers also were overrepresented. Most of the television characters were law-abiding, healthy, and sane individuals. They were most likely to be white Americans (four times out of five), occasionally Europeans, and rarely blacks (only 2 percent of all characters shown during the week).

Within this somewhat distorted portrait of the world, how do the heroes and villains appear? Male dominance continues: heroes outnumber heroines 2 to 1, and villains outnumber villainesses by almost 4 to 1. Heroes are usually younger than villains; the average villainess is older than the average villain;

---

[6] Dallas Smythe, *Three Years of New York Television*, Monitoring Study Number 6 (Urbana, Ill.: National Association of Educational Broadcasters, 1953).

the average heroine is younger than the hero. Smythe suggests that in these portrayals villains represent the menace of the older generation who have more social power than the heroes, but who are physically and sexually on the wane.

White Americans have the edge over foreigners, providing proportionately more of the heroes (83 percent) and fewer of the villains (69 percent). The foreigners who are heroic, however, are more likely to be women than men, whereas among Americans heroes outnumber heroines 3 to 1. Only ten blacks appeared during the week, two as heroic characters and eight in supporting roles, neither heroic nor villainous.

As might be expected, heroes are usually law-abiding and villains lawbreakers. But to say merely that this is expected is to underrate the sociological significance of presenting heroes as supporters of the normative structure of the society. Innovators who by-pass society's laws to achieve their goals are unusual among our heroes and heroines. Robin Hood is the exception in a world in which most heroic characters operate within the law. In television "life," disregard for society's norms is—or, at least, was—usually not heroic but undesirable.

After describing the social characteristics of the heroes and villains, the researchers applied a special technique (called *semantic differentiation*) to explore the apparent personalities of the central characters and the degree of stereotyping in the casting. Specially trained monitors rated each leading character on sixteen scales based on pairs of antonyms. One scale, for example, contained the antonyms "fair" and "unfair." The monitor scored each central character according to whether the character appeared to have the quality of being more fair or unfair. Ten of the scales used were valuative, requiring the judge to rate the character on such qualities as bravery or cowardice, attractiveness or ugliness. Two were measures of "inner power"—strength and hardness. Four referred to such traits as sharpness, quickness, and smartness, considered to be measures of "activity."

Heroes were typically evaluated as having personalities that conformed closely to the ideals of our culture—very brave, attractive, honest, clean, kind, fair, loyal, admirable, and moderately happy and generous. Villains were judged to be almost the direct opposite of the heroes—very ugly, deceitful, cruel, unfair, despicable, and moderately sad, dirty, miserly, and disloyal. Villains were rated slightly more brave than cowardly, but not as brave as heroes. Villains had at least as much inner power as the heroes, however, and were rated almost as high as the heroes in strength and higher in hardness. Heroes tended to be slightly sharper, quicker, and smarter than the villains. With a few exceptions, these general patterns of heroic and villainous personalities applied to both male and female characters.

More recent information on the demographic composition and other qualities of characters on prime-time television drama in America is presented in a continuing research program called "studies of cultural indicators," by communications researcher George Gerbner and his associates.[7] Gerbner places his systematic program of content analysis within the larger framework of a theoretical model of mass communications that encompasses research on production, messages, audiences, and effects. (This underscores our earlier observation that content analysis is only one of a set of approaches to an understanding of mass communications.) Gerbner regards mass communication as the mass production and distribution of messages (comprising message systems) that cultivate the images of society shared by its public. His program of research spans three areas of analysis: institutional process analysis, concerned with mass media; message system analysis, concerned with content; and cultivation analysis, concerned with communication effects. Content analysis, in this context, deals with message systems and their symbolic functions of presenting the social world for the audience in terms of what *is*, what is *important*, what is *right*, and what is *related* to what. The basic theoretical approach has informed content analyses of mass media presentations of mental illness, education, film heroes, news, violence, and other subjects. And since 1967 it has guided a continuing study of violence in television drama.

Gerbner regards television drama as the mainstream of "the symbolic environment cultivating common conceptions of life,

---

[7] See George Gerbner, "Cultural Indicators: The Third Voice," in George Gerbner et al., eds., *Communications Technology and Social Policy* (New York: Wiley, 1973). Also George Gerbner, "Violence in Television Drama: Trends and Symbolic Functions," in *Television and Social Behavior*, Vol. 1, ed. George Comstock and Eli Rubinstein, *Media Content and Control* (Washington, D.C.: U.S. Government Printing Office, 1972).

society, and the world," at least in those societies in which it is prominent.[8] Even though its content may be viewed as entertainment, it nonetheless cultivates, sometimes subtly, synthetic images of life, society, and the world. Therefore, analysis of the content of television drama is a first step toward understanding its potential or real effects on the viewers. Toward this end, systematic content analyses have been made of the nature of the world portrayed on prime-time television drama in the United States during sample weeks from 1967 through 1973. These analyses have documented the demographic casting of characters that populate the world of television drama, their activities, and the social outcomes of these activities, among other items of concern. Special attention has been given to the portrayal of violence, but not merely in terms of its frequency. The most detailed published findings from these studies report on the years 1967–1969, which will serve for our illustration.[9]

American television drama in the late 1960s, as in the early 1950s, reported above, was most likely to place its action in the United States rather than in foreign settings. About three-quarters of the leading characters in television plays were men; very young and very old people were underrepresented in the stories, as were lower-class individuals. About three-quarters of the leading characters were white, and about seven out of ten were Americans.

Comparison of these figures with those from the early 1950s, even allowing for the fact that the sets of studies refer to different kinds of television programs, suggests that the characters in television drama far from duplicate the demographic composition of our society in either decade. What difference does this make? Symbolic representation in the fictional world of television, according to Gerbner, signifies social existence; its absence means symbolic annihilation. Thus one interpretation of the social meaning of demographically distorted life on television is that it is a hidden lesson on who counts in society.

Violence is a common element in American television drama,

---

[8] George Gerbner and Larry Gross, "Cultural Indicators: The Social Reality of Television Drama" (Unpublished research proposal) (Philadelphia: Annenberg School of Communications, 1973), p. 2.

[9] See Gerbner, "Violence in Television Drama."

appearing in more than 70 percent of the dramatic programs under study in the late 1960s. More pertinent to our immediate interests, however, are data on who commits such violence and who are its victims. During the sample weeks of 1967–1969 under study, there was some reduction in the total proportion of violent roles portrayed (due in part to public and governmental concern over violence on television). But these reductions only served to exaggerate previous differences in violent roles portrayed by different kinds of individuals. Men, for example, were more likely to be shown as the perpetrators of violence, and women were more likely to be the victims. Such patterns are interesting in their own right as possible role portrayals for susceptible audience members, but they take on additional significance in terms of their potential symbolic meaning. Gerbner interprets the show of violence, for example, as a symbolic lesson in social power. In the real world, he notes:

Acts of physical violence are rare, a last resort when symbolic means fail. In the symbolic world, overt physical motion makes dramatically visible that which in the real world is usually symbolic and hidden. Thus violence in drama cannot be equated with violence in the real world. Real violence is the dead end of symbolic action. Symbolic violence is one of society's chief instruments for achieving the aims of real violence without having to commit any.[10]

Thus descriptive content analysis, focusing only on the manifest show of violence and its possible direct effects on the audience through such psychological mechanisms as imitation, would miss the latent, sociologically important consequences of such content as symbolic lessons about who are likely to be socially dominant and who are likely to be victims within the culture of a society.

Whether or not the audience is aware of the hidden lessons associated with character casting in television drama cannot be answered by content analysis. Nor can the impact of such portrayals be assessed without other kinds of studies. Nevertheless, scientific and systematic analyses of content such as Lowenthal's qualitative analysis of biographies and Smythe's and Gerbner's quantitative studies of television characters go far in enlarging our knowledge about the heroes of our popular culture. They

10 Ibid., p. 44.

provide us with a factual background against which possible effects can be more realistically considered.

THE WORLD OF WORK

Popular portrayals of people at work, whether the characters are heroic or villainous, provide a potential source of imagery about a social role that everyone must cope with, whether as a performer of the job or through interaction with those who hold such occupations. Information and impressions about occupations provided by the mass media may be the only, or at least a major, learning source for many young people in a society, especially those who are unlikely to know an adult so employed. Therefore, a number of content analyses of television and other mass media have paid particular attention to the numbers, proportions, and kinds of occupations presented; in addition, some studies have examined the personal and social characteristics associated with particular occupations.

Quantitative content analyses of American television drama, such as those by Smythe and by Gerbner, have documented the general overrepresentation of middle-class occupations and the underrepresentation of working-class jobs in comparison with the proportions of individuals so employed in the national labor force. Smythe's study, in addition, presented an analysis of the types of characters cast into various occupational roles. Using the semantic differential scales described above, he examined the personality profiles of such occupational groups as business executives, public officers, criminals, white-collar workers, teachers, lawyers, journalists, doctors, scientists, entertainers, farmers, domestic servants, and housewives. With rare exceptions, all characters holding jobs within the legitimate occupational groups (that is, excluding criminals and illegal business executives) were shown to be more in line with community ideals than not. However, there were wide differences in the characteristics associated with these groups. For example, among the professionals the journalists were most favorably characterized, being especially honest, strong, hard, and quick. Scientists, on the other hand, were rated as the least brave, kind, or fair of the professionals and almost the slowest, dullest, weakest, and softest. Lawyers were rated "dirtiest." Doctors and entertainers had favorable personalities. Among the other groups, only the criminals and illegal business executives had predominantly unfavorable personality characteristics.

Stereotyping of characters was measured in terms of the degree to which the apparent personalities of the members of each group conformed to the typical pattern for that group. By this criterion, journalists were the most stereotyped, doctors were least. Other groups subject to stereotyped portrayals were lawyers, teachers, and law-enforcement officers.

A sociological view of occupational roles as portrayed on television is presented in Melvin De Fleur's analysis of a sample of six months of television programs shown in a Midwestern American community in the mid-1960s.[11] De Fleur argues that children gain insight into the world of work through socialization by accidental and haphazard exposure to many learning sources, including the mass media, among which television is an especially relevant learning source. His content analysis identified each occupational portrayal on the television shows—that is, a person performing some kind of recognizable occupational duty, appearing for at least three minutes during the show. Occupational portrayals were analyzed according to the type of occupation, the background settings of the work, power over other individuals during interactions, and characteristics and traits of the workers.

De Fleur found, as have others, that the world of work on television greatly distorts the real distribution in the labor force; furthermore, it is a man's world, with relatively few women portrayed as gainfully employed. The places of work or dwellings of workers also were studied, as having implications for the style of life supposedly characteristic of a particular occupation. Taken literally, however, such clues proved anomalous, for the most glamorous work settings surrounded persons engaged as personal servants (although lawyers and theatrical agents also ranked relatively high). Despite these anomalies the idea behind this search for the social context of occuptions has merit and holds promise of sociologically interesting insights into the televised world of work.

---

[11] Melvin De Fleur, "Occupational Roles as Portrayed on Television," *Public Opinion Quarterly* 28 (1964): 57–74.

Next De Fleur considered the distribution of power among televised occupations, as indicated by the number of times an individual portraying a particular occupation gave orders to someone else, obeyed an order, gave permission to someone, received permission, received a title of respect, and used a title of respect toward someone else. From these actions an index of power was calculated for each occupational category, and occupations were ranked. Among the occupational groups ranked relatively high on power were foremen, ranch owners, judges, district attorneys, artists, police officials, members of the clergy, and physicians; relatively low were persons in service occupations, office workers, salesmen, semiskilled and unskilled workers, nurses, personal servants, and enlisted military personnel. De Fleur notes that, in terms of power, a criterion regarded by children as important in an occupation, according to supplementary research, television presents least often and as least desirable the middle-level and working-class occupations in which many young viewers are most likely to have to make a living.

Finally, De Fleur analyzed a variety of social and personal characteristics of each worker portrayed on television, such as physical attractiveness, friendliness, neatness of dress, and speech patterns. There was a concentration of negative or positive characteristics among various kinds of workers; physicians, for example, were shown not only as well dressed and socially skilled, but also as handsome. Furthermore, there was considerable stereotyping of occupations; thus lawyers were shown as clever, artists as temperamental, police as hardened and brutal, salesmen as glib.

Less anticipated, however, is De Fleur's observation that television seems to be preoccupied with the atypical aspects of an occupation and its performance. Physicians, for example, rarely are shown treating a routine case of measles; more often they are performing a dramatic operation. These atypical features seem to be the source of the dramatic, interesting, entertaining features of television stories. But to note this is not merely to point up the obvious. For regardless of the function of such dramatic portraits as entertainment, they also have the potential function or dysfunction of presenting distorted views of the world of work and of particular occupations to the viewers, most of whom lack day-to-day realistic experiences of what it is like to do such jobs.

De Fleur concludes that television's treatment of occupational roles is selective, unreal, stereotyped, and misleading. He cautions, however, that content analysis presents only one kind of information to be fitted into the total study of the role of television and other influences in the socialization of individuals into the world of work and other roles. Content analysis needs to be complemented by studies of the viewers' responses to the media and the media's effects upon their beliefs.

Even when evidence is limited to content analysis, however, much can be gleaned from qualitative as well as quantitative observations. A study of the first twenty-five years of the comic strip "Little Orphan Annie," for example, disclosed that blue-collar workers were rarely identified as people with names; rather, they were shown in group and crowd scenes, lacking in individual identity and personality.[12] By contrast, people holding middle-class and upper-class occupations were usually identified by names and played individualistic roles. De Fleur's study notes, almost in passing, that certain occupations rarely or never appeared in the television stories in the early 1960s; scientists are an example. And a content analysis of daytime television serial dramas (soap operas) in 1973 revealed that, although the actors were cast in a variety of occupations, the characters seldom if ever were shown in the process of carrying out any of their occupational tasks.[13] The occupation was a costume for the character, who typically was engaged in personal conversations and activities. Neither characters nor plots centered on the routine tasks and problems of the world of work.

THE VISIBLE MINORITIES

Sociologists, along with others, have directed attention to the symbolic representation of minority-group members in the mass media. Most recently, attention has been focused upon the mass

---

[12] Donald Auster, "A Content Analysis of Little Orphan Annie," *Social Problems* 2 (1954): 26–33.

[13] Mildred Downing, "The Wold of Daytime Television Serial Drama" (Ph.D. diss., University of Pennsylvania, 1974). Also "Heroine of the Daytime Serial," *Journal of Communications* 24 (1974): 130–137.

media's treatment of women and blacks. Content analyses have sometimes been undertaken because of the researcher's concern with the social problem of discrimination and prejudice against minority peoples along racial, ethnic, religious, and other lines. Symbolic underrepresentation, misrepresentation, stereotyping, and other forms of distorted portrayals of minority individuals may, it is argued, contribute to prejudicial and discriminatory treatments of individuals in real life. In addition, these symbolic portraits may be the major sources of impressions and information that certain people have about others (for instance, many white suburban children have little or no direct contact with blacks). Media portrayals also provide potential role models for the audience members, and the quantity and quality of minority-group portrayals may have important consequences for the mass media's impact on socialization, especially for the young. These social and theoretical reasons, among others, have prompted a relatively large number of content analyses about minorities in the mass media during the past thirty to forty years.

An early example of the use of content analysis for the study of potentially prejudicial and discriminatory treatment of minorities in popular communications media is a study by Bernard Berelson and Patricia Salter of the presentation of majority and minority Americans in our magazine fiction during the late 1930s and early 1940s.[14] The researchers found that the characters in these popular magazine short stories were mainly white Protestant Americans with no distinguishable foreign ancestors; less than one out of ten characters were Anglo-Saxon and Scandinavian minorities and foreigners; and about one out of ten were Jews, blacks, Orientals, and other minorities and foreigners. Minority and foreign characters tended to be described stereotypically, as in the case of the Italian gangster. Native Americans also were more likely to be shown as engaged in pleasanter and more desirable work than others. Minority-group members were more likely than others to be shown in subordinate occupational roles, as servants, for example, and in general were not accorded equality with majority Americans in such social interactions as

---

[14] Bernard Berelson and Patricia Salter, "Majority and Minority Americans: An Analysis of Magazine Fiction," *Public Opinion Quarterly* 10, (1946): 168–190.

courtship and marriage. The authors note that even though minorities were not overtly depreciated in the stories, a subtle form of discrimination appeared through the presentation of "different classes of citizenship for different classes of people." Times change, of course, and it is not our point that this early study reflects the treatment of minorities in magazine fiction today; rather, we present the study as an example of the kinds of questions to which such content analyses are often addressed.

One sign of changing times is the increased visibility of members of minority groups in roles on television programs. As John Seggar and Penny Wheeler, the authors of a content analysis of ethnic and sex representation in television drama, observed in 1971, "When viewing television today, it is hard to believe that depictions of minority group members were a rarity just 10 to 15 years ago. The inclusion, for example, of a black actor or actress was almost sure to produce a controversy."[15] We have noted above that Smythe's content analysis of a week of television drama during the early 1950s found that only 2 percent of the characters were blacks and that only about one character out of every three was a woman. Gerbner's analyses of prime-time television drama for 1967–1969 found that about three-quarters of the leading characters were white and three-quarters were men. Seggar and Wheeler, in their study of television dramas in modern settings in 1971, found that 75 percent of the characters were white Americans and about 6 percent were black Americans (the remainder being various other minorities).[16] Four of every five characters were men. The study focused on the portrayal of majority- and minority-group members in various occupational roles and compared these figures with the proportions of each group in such occupations as recorded in the United States Census Reports. In general, television portrayals of all ethnic groups overrepresented professional, technical, and service occupations and underrepresented farm managers, clerical workers, service workers, craftsmen, operators, farm laborers, and laborers. Minorities were more likely than majority white Americans to be concentrated in personal service jobs. Both

[15] John Seggar and Penny Wheeler, "World of Work on TV: Ethnic and Sex Representation in TV Drama," *Journal of Broadcasting* 17 (1973): 201–214.
[16] Ibid.

men and women were shown in stereotypic occupational roles, but females more so than males.

That television's stereotyping by sex in occupational roles is not limited to dramatic programs is suggested by a content analysis, by Joseph Dominick and Gail Rauch, of the image of women in network television commercials shown in New York City during early 1971.[17] The men in these television commercials were cast into forty-three different occupations, the women into eighteen. More than half the women were shown in the role of housewife or mother; one in every seven men was portrayed primarily as a husband or father.

Further examples could be added, but those cited should be sufficient to illustrate the usual form of such content analyses and their typical results. Certain minorities have become more visible on American television and perhaps in other mass media content. To note this is to add little more than might be obvious to the casual observer of today's mass communications. But the studies serve to document the extent of this visibility with greater precision and on a more representative set of data than can be done through casual observation. Furthermore, when extended over time through replications carried out by comparable procedures, these studies allow the detection and the measurement of trends in mass-communicated portrayals of minority groups and social roles, thereby providing a running indicator of our changing symbolic world. We caution again, however, that interpretations of such findings, either to draw inferences about causes or about effects, cannot be supported through content analyses alone.

GOALS, MEANS, AND CONSEQUENCES

Two components of culture that are of special interest to sociologists are socially valued goals and socially prescribed or disapproved means for achieving these goals. This sociological interest has carried over into a few content analyses of mass communications, in which the mass media are regarded as common sources from which people may learn about their own society and its culture, as well as about other societies. In the

---

[17] Joseph Dominick and Gail Rauch, "The Image of Women in Network TV Commercials," *Journal of Broadcasting* 16 (1972): 259–265.

view of one team of sociologists who have studied television programs:

Such content analyses may be particularly fruitful when they work with problems and categories designed to discover underlying values repeatedly portrayed in a wide variety of settings and situations. . . . We may postulate that effects are more likely to emerge over time to the extent that such programs deal in *patterned ways* with basic goals and the mechanisms for their achievement since a consistent portrayal of these affords the maximum opportunity for reinforcement.[18]

In order to follow this promising line of sociological investigation, content analyses must be fashioned to discover the goals portrayed by the mass media, the approved and disapproved methods for achieving these goals, the degree to which these methods are shown to be successful or unsuccessful ways of achieving goals, and other consequences that follow from using such means. Few quantitative content analyses combine information in this fashion. An interesting exception is the aforementioned study of television programs by sociologists Otto Larsen, Louis Gray, and J. Gerald Fortis.[19] It is impossible to know, without further research, whether the findings from this study, based upon a content analysis of evening television network entertainment programs shown in Seattle in the early 1960s, would apply elsewhere today. The study nonetheless stands as an instructive example of this kind of content analysis.

Observers recorded the frequency with which each of eight kinds of goals were portrayed in the programs under study; some of the goals were desires for property, self-preservation, affection, and power. Eight classes of methods for goal achievement also were identified and recorded; some of the methods were legal methods, economic methods, violence, and chance. Three kinds of programs were examined, each more or less likely to be viewed by children: adult programs, "kidult" programs, and children's programs. By comparing the relative frequency with which various goals and methods appear in these three types

---

[18] Otto Larsen, Louis Gray, and J. Gerald Fortis, "Goals and Goal-Achievement Methods in Television Content: Models for Anomie?" *Sociological Inquiry* 33 (1963): 180–196. Quotation is from pp. 180–181.

[19] Ibid.

of programs, it was possible to see whether children and adults were being exposed to different "cultural lessons." In general, they were not, although there are exceptions.

Particular theoretical significance is given to the combination of goals and means for achieving them. These means were grouped into three categories according to whether they are generally socially approved (for example, legal), socially disapproved (for example, violence), or either (for example, chance). An analysis was made of the extent to which characters were shown as successful or unsuccessful in achieving each of the eight types of goals when following socially approved, disapproved, or neutral methods. The findings suggest that conduct that is *not* socially approved seemed to be portrayed by television as having a better chance of success than methods that are socially approved. This finding appeared to hold generally, regardless of the particular goal sought or the type of program on which it was portrayed. The researchers relate these findings to the larger sociological concern with social *anomie*, a condition characterized by Robert Merton as a cultural emphasis upon the successful achievement of goals through expedient means with an accompanying withdrawal of emphasis upon socially approved means—a state of relative normlessness, in which "anything goes."[20] According to these researchers, television dramatic programing appears consistently to portray a state of anomie, in which socially approved goals are often achieved by unsanctioned means. The researchers hasten to add, however, that content analysis cannot determine whether the television audience perceives this pattern or is influenced by it; such questions can be addressed only through direct studies of the audience. The authors also note that other researchers have asserted that the mass media tend to support the common values and mores of the culture, thereby contributing to social stability and maintenance of social norms. In all likelihood the media do both. Further research needs to consider the degree to which various mass communications suggest normlessness or social conformity, the conditions under which media give emphasis to one or the other, the manner in which such patterns are conveyed, and, of

---

[20] Robert K. Merton. *Social Theory and Social Structure* (Glencoe, Ill.: Free Press, 1957) Chs. 4 and 5.

course, their consequences for the society and its members.

Further attention to the possible connections between mass media content and social anomie seems warranted. The absence of such research, however, ought not to preclude theoretically relevant speculation about it. We choose, therefore, to close this section by suggesting an approach to the problem that takes a somewhat different tack from that of Larsen and his colleagues but that is not necessarily contradictory to theirs. Central to our approach is Robert Merton's conceptualization of anomie, mentioned briefly above.

Merton regards anomie as a breakdown in the cultural structure—the organized set of normative values governing behavior, common to members of a society. Anomie is likely to occur when there is an "acute disjunction" between the cultural goals and norms, on the one hand, and the group members' socially structured capacities to follow them, on the other hand. To oversimplify, cultural strains occur when various segments of the society either cannot abide by the social norms prescribing ways to achieve desired goals or, upon following them, seldom if ever succeed; concurrently, individuals appear to succeed by means counter to the social norms. In such situations success seems to justify the means, and a sense of amorality, even cynicism, prevails. Anything goes if it succeeds.

Given a cultural pattern that stresses success, for example, in terms of wealth, without a corresponding emphasis upon legitimate means for achieving it, how do individuals behave? Merton suggests five types of role adaptation to the cultural pattern and examines how the social structure operates to encourage, even to pressure, individuals to follow one or another of these modes of adaptation. The typology refers to role behavior with regard to specific cultural spheres of different goals and norms and is not a classification of personalities. An individual may make one kind of adaptation with regard to the goal of financial success, for example, and a different adaptation with regard to the goal of love or of salvation. The typology classifies adaptations according to whether the individual accepts or rejects a culturally approved goal and whether the individual accepts or rejects the institutionally approved means for achieving that goal. Five types are suggested:

1. *Conformity*, the most common behavior in a stable society, signifies acceptance of both the goal and the socially approved methods for its achievement.
2. *Ritualism* refers to an abandonment of the goal for oneself but a strict adherence to the norms about how to achieve it (for example, continuing to believe in hard work and thriftiness, even though one no longer hopes that they will lead to a fortune).
3. *Innovation* refers to personal acceptance of a goal but without equal concern for the approved means (for example, acquiring wealth through crime).
4. *Retreatism* is signified by an abandonment of a goal and the sanctioned means (for example, "dropping out" of economic competition by becoming a hobo).
5. *Rebellion* is characterized by the rejection of an established goal and its accompanying norms, combined with an effort to substitute an alternative goal and new normative procedures not only for oneself but for other members of the society, perhaps for the total society.

All adaptations except conformity may be regarded as socially deviant and hence threatening to the established culture, each undermining it in some fashion. But it is possible that innovation, retreatism, and rebellion hold the greatest potential for fostering social anomie, since they provide visible signs of rejection or violation of socially approved norms for conduct.

In relation to the topic of mass communications content, one may question the degree to which the mass media portray each of these five styles of role adaptation and the consequences that appear to accompany them. Answers are not easy to come by. Separate sets of questions would have to be framed for each of the several major social goals portrayed, covering different spheres of life. And findings might differ according to the various media and types of content under analysis. The extent to which social conformity is the predominant role model portrayed for any sphere of social activities might reflect the conservative role of the media in preserving cultural patterns. Deviant role adaptations, unless portrayed as unsuccessful or as leading to other undesirable consequences, are potentially dysfunctional.

There is reason to believe that the mass media tend to convey common values to members of the society. The goal of financial success, for example, has appeared frequently in studies of such diverse American media as comic strips, television drama, popular magazine fiction, and popular biographies. The mass media also provide explicit or implicit lessons about the institutionalized norms of behavior. And there is verisimilitude in much mass media content, ranging from the apparent objectivity of news coverage to the contemporary and realistic settings of many television dramas. It does not seem unreasonable, then, to suggest that much of mass communication's content purports to reflect life, albeit in dramatized and stylized forms at times. To the extent that this is so, it also seems plausible that the media portraits of society have an impact on the audience's beliefs about their chances of success in achieving life goals and about the extent to which social conformity or alternate forms of deviant role behavior are common and successful in the society. The media thereby may contribute to people's perception of society as more or less moral, more or less normless and anomic.

One critical point for consideration is how the mass media manage the problem of failure. To the extent that the media give the appearance of reflecting reality, they must cope with the fact that conformity to social norms does not always lead to success for the individual or for significant segments of the society. How is this discrepancy between cultural prescriptions and social reality handled? What kinds of role behavior are portrayed as adaptations to failure? What patterned mechanisms are employed to manage the problem? Here are some sociologically promising questions for future content analyses.

It seems plausible that systematic research will show that the bulk of mass-communicated content supports conformity in social behavior. This support might be explicit in the stories and their featured characters or implicit in the taken-for-granted background of characters and activities against which the major drama, news, and non-fiction events are played out. Most characters in stories conduct their lives in an apparently "normal" way. If in pursuit of love, they court rather than buy their loved one. Men and women try to appear attractive and respectable in fashion, although styles may vary. The need to work and to earn pay or profit is almost the universal lot, not only for the majority of law-abiding citizens but even for many engaged in questionable or illegal livelihoods ("This gun *for hire!*").

I suspect, too, that the media tend to emphasize preservation of the social norms for good behavior even in the face of failure to achieve the ultimate goals—that ritualism is the next most commonly encouraged form of role adaptation. Ritualism can be encouraged through such symbolic mechanisms as goal reduction, goal substitution, goal diversion, and the hand of fate. We will illustrate each mechanism (the terms are our own) through findings from diverse content analyses.

A good example of goal reduction appears in Donald Auster's content analysis of twenty-five years of the comic strip "Little Orphan Annie."[21] Auster considered, among other things, the treatment given to the goal of business success and prescriptions for achieving it. At one point Annie contrasts the wealthy Daddy Warbucks with a lesser character, Spike, who had not done so well financially, and she provides a rationalization for those who are less successful. Daddy, she explains, was willing to take long chances, to play for high stakes, and he won. Spike, on the other hand, liked security, small towns, and a quiet life, but he nevertheless worked hard. He never achieved wealth, but by the age of forty this "failure" owned his own small business, his own home, and some ground. Annie concludes that people "with not too much" are happy to think how much better off they are, with a little, than the very rich are. She does not point out that the goals of both characters are qualitatively the same—material and financial gain—although the threshold of success has been scaled down for the man whose labors never produced a fortune.

Our example of goal substitution is taken from an analysis of values in popular magazine fiction by P. Johns-Heine and Hans Gerth.[22] The authors compared, among other things, success as portrayed in stories in the *Saturday Evening Post* during the decades prior to and immediately following the beginning of the great economic depression of the 1930s. (The number of cases

---

[21] Auster, "A Content Analysis of Little Orphan Annie."

[22] Patrick Johns-Heine and Hans Gerth, "Values in Mass Periodical Fiction, 1921–1940," *Public Opinion Quarterly* 13 (1949): 105–113.

is small, and, as with Auster's analysis, we present the case only as an illustration of the mechanism, not as evidence.) The authors report that in the success stories of the 1920s it was common for men of proven ambition and achievement to be rewarded by social ascent. Heroes in the 1930s also were "good" men, virtuous and hard working. But these qualities no longer were shown as leading to the goal of social ascent; rather, they more commonly led to other rewards: love and esteem from one's fellow men, certainly socially worthwhile goals. The lesson appears to be: continue to adhere to the norms—not because they are likely to lead to the social goals of the past, but because they will lead to equally desirable goals of the present. Virtue becomes its own reward.

To illustrate our third mechanism, goal diversion, we refer back to Lowenthal's analysis of popular biographies and to the quotation cited from it earlier in this chapter. Lowenthal's example suggests that the very definition and meaning of success, the framework within which its consequences were judged and valued, has shifted from achievement and social contribution to emphasis upon the consumer behavior and private life styles of celebrities and popular heroes. The audience, he suggests, can compare itself favorably with these successful heroes when being successful seems to mean being able to choose a brand of cigarettes, prefer a particular beer or whiskey, wear a golf shirt, enjoy leisure-time pursuits, and so on. Such symbols of success lend themselves to scaling down to fit the means of many individuals. Their acquisition becomes semantically defined as success; hence the diversion.

The hand-of-fate mechanism encourages ritualism by making compliance with the social norms appear to be a necessary but not sufficient condition for success. It does this through the introduction of such uncontrollable catalytic conditions as luck, "the break," intuition, and the helping hand.

In terms of Merton's other types of role adaptation, occasionally the media may appear to reward innovative behavior. But this seems rare and reserved for individuals likely to be identified as extraordinary characters. More frequently, innovation is portrayed as a costly deviation from custom. A content analysis of themes in women's magazines during the early twentieth century, for example, showed that material and financial success was a goal for many female characters.[23] But the socially approved method for achieving this, at that time, was through a successful, "sensible" marriage, rewarded by love, in which the woman's role was to bring out the latent qualities in her husband, inspiring him to achieve success for the family. Less acceptable as a method for a woman was to make her own way in a career. Stories depicting career women were restricted to cases of eminent success, success achieved at the price of suffering, lack of love, and lack of affection. The career woman was an innovator, within the law but at the edge of violating social folkways if not mores, and she paid the price.

More recently, Helen Franzwa reports on a content analysis of the major female characters in a sample of women's magazine fiction from 1940–1970. About three out of every five of these women characters were not working outside the home. About nine out of every ten working women held middle-status or lower-status jobs, seen as temporary roles to be forsaken upon marriage, an actively sought life-goal. Those few women for whom work and careers appeared important paid the price in a concomitant disintegration of their home lives, by never marrying, or by suffering divorce.[24]

Retreatism, when portrayed, seems likely to be either a comic or a tragic happening. When comic, the character may have certain redeeming social virtues, as does Charlie Chaplin's sympathetic bum. More likely, the deviant is shown as a problem case, for example, escaping responsibilities through alcohol, dropping out with drugs, drifting. Rebellion is perhaps potentially the most threatening form of role adaptation, seeking as it does to change the existing culture (and society) rather than to accommodate to it. It may be presented as the stuff of heroes. But if so, I suspect that they are mainly historically legitimized heroes. Or, if they are contemporary characters, they are likely to be shown calling us to return to earlier acceptable (even

---

[23] Ibid.

[24] Helen H. Franzwa, "Working Women in Fact and Fiction," *Journal of Communication* 24 (1974): 104–109. See this issue also for other reports on women in the media, including content analyses of women in television commercials, prime-time television drama, television cartoons, and daytime serials.

"higher") social values from a world turned amoral or anomic, if not evil.

These are but speculations. The reader may well form different impressions about this facet of our popular culture. Answers can come only from future research. Our point is to illustrate one direction in which a sociologically informed approach to content analysis might enrich our understanding of popular culture and some possible functions and dysfunctions for society and its members. An approach of this sort, although difficult to carry out with precision and reliability, carries us a step beyond descriptive, quantitative accounts of mass-communicated topics, characters, and specific conduct such as acts of violence.

The studies selected for review in this chapter provide a partial analysis of the cultural content of American mass communications. They do not, as previously noted, provide evidence about any of the effects of this content on the audience. We now turn, in the final chapter, to this general question of the social effects of mass communications.

social effects
of mass
communications

Anyone who wants to invite a quarrel about mass communications need only assert an opinion about their social effects. Charges, denials, and countercharges color almost every public discussion about media impact in the editorial columns of our daily newspapers, in testimonies before Senate committees, in critical essays in journals of opinion, and elsewhere. Typical controversial questions are: Does the show of violence and crime in movies and on television harm children, even to the extent of causing juvenile delinquency? Does pornography lead to sexually deviant and other antisocial behavior? Can adult information campaigns raise the level of public knowledge about national and international issues? Can the mass media be used to persuade persons to safeguard their health through checkups for cancer, venereal disease, heart ailments, and other disorders? Can a newspaper crusade swing an election? Does international communication help to prevent war? Widely different opinions can be found on each of these and similar questions involving the effects of mass media on public taste, morals, health behavior, politics, adult education, crime, and other social matters. Perhaps only within the restrictive framework of scientific discussions are such topics handled with dispassion, and even there tempers sometimes flare.

REASONS FOR THE CONTROVERSY OVER EFFECTS

Why is there so much public controversy about these matters? Two major reasons are the shortage of conclusive scientific evidence on media effects and the tone of social urgency that often surrounds the question about effects.

Scientific research on communications effects, despite some recent massive efforts, remains far too scarce and the results of research are too inconclusive to provide the information needed for definitive answers to the socially pressing questions. As one scholar testified back in 1955 concerning the controversy over television's effects on children, "The effect of television on children is controversial not because some people are against crime and others for it; it is controversial because so little is known that anyone can inject his prejudices or his views into the debate without being proven wrong."[1] Twenty years later, the available research findings are still far from unequivocal, especially if one tries to interpret them as evidence for or against particular courses of social action. As an example, a three-year, $1 million program of studies on the effects of television on social behavior was conducted from 1969–1971 on behalf of the United States surgeon general. The report from this program summarizes the issue about the effects of televised violence upon viewers as follows:

It is entirely possible that some types of extensive portrayals of violence could reduce the propensity to violence in society and that some types might increase it. In our present state of knowledge, we are not able to specify what kinds of violence portrayal will have what net result on society. . . . the key question that we should be asked is thus a complicated one concerning alternatives. The proper question is, "What kinds of changes, if any, in television content and practices could have a significant net effect in reducing the propensity to undesirable aggression among the audience, and what other effects, desirable and undesirable, would each such change have?" . . . The state of present knowledge does not permit an agreed answer.[2]

---

[1] Paul Lazarsfeld, "Why Is So Little Known About the Effects of TV and What Can Be Done?" *Public Opinion Quarterly* 19 (Fall 1955): 243–251.

[2] Surgeon General's Scientific Advisory Committee on Television and Social Behavior, *Television and Growing Up: The Impact of Televised Violence* (Washington, D.C.: U.S. Government Printing Office, 1972), pp. 4–5.

Often there is a tone of social urgency in discussions about the effects of mass media, especially concerning such salient and insistent social problems as juvenile delinquency, violence, crime, and public morality. This social anxiety makes people impatient with a slow, objective, and dispassionate scientific orientation toward the problems and encourages a search for immediate opinions and social remedies.

Sometimes the mass media themselves are perceived as social problems by laymen and social critics, a turn of events worth examination. Paul Lazarsfeld and Robert K. Merton have identified four sources of the public's concern about mass media.[3] First, many people are alarmed by the mass media's ubiquity and potential power to manipulate people for good or evil. The average person feels that he or she has little or no control over this power. Second, some people fear that economic interest groups may use the mass media to ensure public conformity to the social and economic status quo, thus minimizing social criticism and weakening the audience's capacity for critical thinking. Third, critics argue that the mass media, in accommodating large audiences, may cause a deterioration of aesthetic tastes and popular cultural standards. Finally, some people criticize the mass media as having nullified social gains for which reformers have worked for decades. For instance, through the cumulative effort of many men and women, people at last have shorter working hours, greater opportunities for free education, and social security benefits. Presumably, these are the conditions necessary for enjoying the fine arts, acquiring more education, studying our cultural heritage. But what do many people do with their newly acquired leisure time? They view comedy and variety shows on television, listen to rock or country music on the radio, and go to crime and horror movies. Hence leisure time and its uses pose new "social problems" to be solved.

The absence of definitive research on the social effects of mass communication and the presence of public (sometimes national) concern over the issues involved make the need for additional sociological research especially pressing. At this time any conclu-

---

[3] "Mass Communication, Popular Taste and Organized Social Action," in *The Communication of Ideas*, ed. L. Bryson (New York: Harper & Brothers, 1948).

sions about social consequences must be provisional. Our treatment of the topics in the following sections is admittedly selective. Several comprehensive reviews of the literature on effects are listed in the Selected Readings, however, for the reader who wishes to explore any topic more thoroughly.

EFFECTS OF PORNOGRAPHY AND THE PORTRAYAL OF VIOLENCE

Two themes that generally raise public anxiety and concern when treated by the mass media are sexual activities and violence. Sometimes concern is expressed because the portrayals offend community standards of good taste. But often public anxiety stems from the belief that such content has harmful social, psychological, and moral effects, especially on young people, and leads to antisocial behavior. Public concern is, however, by no means limited to the effects of the media on children and adolescents.

Both sex and violence have been the subjects of several recent federally sponsored commissions on the effects of mass communications, in addition to numerous other less programatic investigations. In 1967 Congress created a Commission on Obscenity and Pornography, whose findings were reported to the President and to the Congress in 1970.[4] In 1968 President Johnson formed a National Commission on the Causes and Prevention of Violence. A Task Force on Mass Media and Violence published a staff report to this commission in 1970.[5] And in 1969 the secretary of health, education, and welfare authorized the formation of a surgeon general's Scientific Advisory Committee on Television and Social Behavior (in response to a request from Senator John O. Pastore) to investigate scientifically the harmful effects, if any, of televised crime and violence, particularly in leading to antisocial behavior and especially by children. The results of this investigation, reported in six vol-

---

[4] Commission on Obscenity and Pornography, *Report* (Washington, D.C.: U.S. Government Printing Office, 1970) See also edition published by Random House, 1970, and paperback edition by Bantam Books, 1970.

[5] David Lange, Robert Baker, and Sandra Ball, *Mass Media and Violence: A Report to the National Commission on the Causes and Prevention of Violence*, Vol. XI (Washington, D.C.: U.S. Government Printing Office, 1969).

umes, were published in 1972.[6] Further research, inspired by these various commission reports, continues on the subject.

Public opinion is divided and inconsistent about the presumed effects of viewing or reading erotic materials. A national survey in 1970, sponsored by the Commission on Obscenity and Pornography found that about two-thirds of American adults believe that sexual materials excite people sexually; about one-half of the public believes that such materials lead people to commit rape; and a little more than one-third of the public believes that sexual materials make people "sex crazy." But six of every ten adults believe that sexual materials provide information about sex; about half think that they improve sex relations of some married couples; about a third think that they provide an outlet for bottled up impulses. Other surveys cited by the Commission indicate that experts also differ from one another in their views. Police chiefs, for example, are much more likely than other professional workers in such fields as child guidance and psychology to believe that reading obscene books plays a significant role in causing juvenile delinquency.[7]

The commission established an "Effects Panel" to review and evaluate existing research on the effects of exposure to sexual stimuli, to design and implement a program of new research, and to summarize and evaluate the total findings for the commission.

---

[6] In addition to *Television and Growing Up*, cited above, the other reports are *Television and Social Behavior*, Reports and Papers, Vol. I: *Media Content and Control*, ed. George Comstock and Eli Rubinstein; Vol. II: *Television and Social Learning*, ed. John Murray, E. Rubinstein, and G. Comstock; Vol. III: *Television and Adolescent Aggressiveness*, ed. G. Comstock and E. Rubinstein; Vol. IV: *Television in Day-to-Day Life: Patterns of Use*, ed. E. Rubinstein, G. Comstock, and J. Murray; Vol. V: *Television's Effects: Further Explorations*, ed. G. Comstock, E. Rubinstein, and J. Murray. All volumes are published by the U.S. Government Printing Office (1972). A useful review apears in Leo Bogart, "Warning: The Surgeon General Has Determined that TV Violence is Moderately Dangerous to Your Child's Mental Health," *Public Opinion Quarterly* 26 (Winter 1972–1973): 491–521. The Committee also published an annotated bibliography on research focusing on television's impact on children, *Television and Social Behavior*, ed. Charles Atkin, John Murray, and Oguz Nayman, listed as Public Health Service Publication No. 2099 (1971). See also Robert Liebert, John Neale, and Emily Davidson, *The Early Window: Effects of Television on Children and Youth* (Elmsford, N.Y.: Pergamon, 1973).

[7] Commission on Obscenity and Pornography, *Report*. See especially pp. 187–197 of the Bantam edition.

The panel's investigation included a variety of research studies, such as several sample surveys of different populations, quasi-experimental studies, studies of the rates and incidence of behavioral responses to sexual stimuli, and controlled experiments. As a result of these studies and prior research findings, the panel concluded that there is reason to doubt that erotica is a determinant of the extent or nature of individuals' habitual sexual behavior. The findings also suggest that exposure to erotica has no independent impact upon character. Research "provides no substantial basis for the belief that erotic materials constitute a primary or significant cause of the development of character deficits or that they operate as a significant determinative factor in causing crime and delinquency."[8] On the basis of these and other findings the commission recommended that "federal, state, and local legislation prohibiting the sale, exhibition, or distribution of sexual materials to consenting adults should be repealed."[9] At the same time, they recommended legislation to protect young persons and others from having sexual materials thrust upon them without their consent through the mails or through open public display. These conclusions themselves were so controversial that only twelve of the eighteen members of the commission subscribed to the recommendations. Some members remained unconvinced that erotic materials had no harmful social effects; others felt that there was no support for any restrictions upon such media content, even for the young. Hence the public debate continues, not having been settled by the evidence from available research.

Public opinion about the effects of the depiction of violence in the mass media is no less divided than that concerning erotica. Gallup Polls taken in the mid-twentieth century found that about seven of every ten Americans believed that juvenile delinquency can be blamed at least partially on such media as crime comic books and mystery programs on television and radio. But three of ten people did not share this opinion; and even if they did, consensus on the matter need not mean that public opinion is correct. Experts likewise disagree.[10] Much of the disagreement

---

[8] Ibid., pp. 286–287

[9] Ibid., p. 57.

[10] Cited in U.S., Congress, Senate, Committee on the Judiciary, *Television and Juvenile Delinquency, Interim Report of the Subcommittee to Investigate Juvenile Delinquency*, 84th Cong., 2nd sess. 1956.

among professionals centers on whether there is any significant connection between media exposure to violence and subsequent delinquent behavior and, if so, whether the connection is causal, contributory, or deterrent.

Some authorities are convinced that certain mass media content have harmful effects that are so obvious as to be self-evident. Fredric Wertham, a well-known psychiatrist, several years ago made the following comment on certain comic books:

They contain such details as one girl squirting fiery "radium dust" on the protruding breasts of another girl ("I think I've discovered your Achilles heel, chum."); white men banging natives around; a close up view of the branded breast of a girl; a girl about to be blinded. Whenever I see a book like this in the hands of a little seven-year-old boy, his eyes glued to the printed page, I feel like a fool to have to prove that this kind of thing is not good mental nourishment for children![11]

Other professionals, who have reservations about mass media's contribution to delinquency, are worried lest too much public alarm about mass media divert attention from such other possible causes of delinquency as disturbed family relationships, the influence of neighborhood gangs, individual emotional disturbances, and insecurity. *Television and Growing Up*, the 1971 report for the U.S. surgeon general on television and social behavior, states that

the real issue is once again quantitative: how much contribution to the violence of our society is made by extensive violent television viewing by our youth? The evidence (or more accurately, the difficulty of finding evidence) suggests that the effect is small compared with many other possible causes, such as parental attitudes or knowledge of and experience with the real violence of our society.[12]

One alternative view is that communication content that to the observer seems harmful actually might be functioning as a deterrent of delinquency—permitting youth to work off their aggressions vicariously, for example, as they watch scenes of

---

[11] Fredric Wertham, *Seduction of the Innocent* (New York: Rinehart and Company, 1954), p. 31. Reprinted by permission of Holt, Rinehart & Winston, Inc.
[12] *Television and Growing Up*, p. 4.

violence on television. This viewpoint was advanced in the studies by psychologists Seymour Feshbach and Robert Singer described in the surgeon general's report on television and social behavior. Other researchers, however, have challenged the "catharsis" hypothesis, and the surgeon general's report concludes:

As matters now stand [in 1971], the weight of the experimental evidence from the present series of studies, as well as from prior research, suggests that viewing filmed violence has an observable effect on some children in the direction of increasing their aggressive behavior. Many of the findings, however, fail to show any statistically significant effects in either direction.[13]

Another viewpoint, shared by many professionals, is that such materials may affect individuals differently. The average adolescent may be unharmed by scenes of violence, but an emotionally disturbed child or a gang may be stimulated by them or have delinquent tendencies reinforced. Thus the surgeon general's report on television summarizes the results of its program of experimental and survey research as follows:

The two sets of findings converge in three respects: a preliminary and tentative indication of a causal relation between viewing violence on television and aggressive behavior; an indication that any such causal relation operates only on some children (who are predisposed to be aggressive); and an indication that it operates only in some environmental contexts.[14]

The surgeon general's report, it should be noted, was not without its critics. Some scientists, including certain investigators who participated in the studies on which the report was based, believe that the evidence warrants a stronger, positive statement about the causal linkage between violent programs and juvenile aggression. Others have suggested that the inquiry failed to address itself to the most meaningful questions. Sociologist Leo

---

[13] Ibid., p. 67. For results of another set of field experiments, in which alternative versions of a television program were shown in order to test their effects on imitative behavior, see Stanley Milgram and R. Lance Shotland, *Television and Anti-Social Behavior* (New York: Academic Press, 1973).

[14] *Television and Growing Up*, p. 11.

Bogart, for example, suggests that the committee's underlying question, "Does exposure to TV violence lead children to specific acts of antisocial behavior?" does not reflect the most fruitful social and sociological orientation to the problem, couched as it is in a stimulus-response paradigm. In real life, Bogart argues, "communications do not work that way. The entire history of mass communications research has shown the tremendous difficulty of teasing out specific effects from the tissue of surrounding social influences. . . . The 'invisible' effects of individual incidents of TV violence might add up to patterns that would leave their traces upon the culture even when specific episodes could not be related to specific effects." The significant questions, he suggests, "go beyond the short-run relationship between television violence and aggressive behavior in children. They concern the long-run influence of the mass media in shaping our national character."[15] Stated another way, they relate to questions of the mass media's role in socialization in our present-day culture, a point to which we shall return shortly.

Finally, some people consider that the risk of certain communications' being harmful is great enough to warrant social control, even though there is inadequate scientific evidence on the subject. As an example, the United States Supreme Court recently expressed the view that state legislatures may constitutionally enact legislation against obscenity in mass communications without scientific data conclusively demonstrating that such materials have harmful effects. In *Kaplan v. California* (1973) the Court held that "States need not wait until behavioral experts or educators can provide empirical data before enacting controls of commerce in obscene materials unprotected by the First Amendment or by a constitutional right to privacy."[16] And in *Paris Adult Theatre I v. Slaton* (1973) the Court stated:

The sum of experience including that of the past two decades, affords an ample basis for legislatures to conclude that a sensitive, key relationship of human existence, central to family life, community welfare,

---

[15] Bogart, "Warning," pp. 518 and 519.
[16] Cited in Michael Goldstein, Harold Kant, and John Hartmen, *Pornography and Sexual Deviance* (Berkeley and Los Angeles: University of California Press, 1973), pp. 162–163.

and the development of human personality, can be debased and distorted by crass commercial exploitation of sex. Nothing in the Constitution prohibits a State from reaching such a conclusion and acting on it legislatively simply because there is no conclusive evidence or empirical data.[17]

Hence social action does not wait upon scientific evidence, here as in other pressing areas of social policy.

Since the views on the effect of mass media on antisocial behavior in general, and on delinquency in particular, are so divergent and the present evidence so inconclusive, it seems best to avoid a premature judgment on this complicated issue and to turn instead to the broader question of *how* the media might influence the total character of youth.

Public attention often centers on two methods by which the mass media seem to affect youth. First, certain content might *overstimulate* the audience, as through scenes about sex, passion, and violence. When such content violates public norms it often becomes the object of reform movements, sometimes within the communications industry itself. For example, one of the earliest publicized reforms of the comic book industry under its first "czar" was a regulation against exaggerated portrayals of women's breasts and other physical characteristics on comic book covers. A second charge is that certain mass communications encourage deviant behavior by children who *imitate* the actions of the characters. The impact of the media in leading to imitative behavior, especially aggressive and violent behavior, has been studied experimentally by a number of psychologists. Indeed, most such research is more psychologically than sociologically oriented; sociologists tend to stress mechanisms of social influence other than stimulus-response or direct imitation. Often the popular belief in imitation is documented by references to stories such as that of a youngster who hanged himself amid comic books portraying such behavior or a child injured or killed while trying to fly like superman. Admittedly, such cases are the exception rather than the rule; not all children who read about hanging attempt it on themselves or other children. But they dramatize a media influence that needs further analysis and research: the possibility that some (and perhaps all) children

---

[17] Ibid., p. 163.

learn something about life and how to cope with it from the mass media. More formally, these cases direct our attention to the sociologically relevant question of the role mass media play in the *socialization* of children and adults.

MASS COMMUNICATION AND SOCIALIZATION

Socialization is the process by which the individual acquires the culture of his or her group and internalizes (in some measure) its social norms, thus leading the person to take into account the expectations of others. It is important to emphasize that socialization is never "total" and is an ongoing process—extending from childhood through old age. Some norms, such as basic rules about food and eating, are transmitted to the individual as a child; others, such as norms about courting, are postponed until later. Some matters involve continuous instruction throughout life. Responsibility for socialization is ordinarily located in specific people or institutions, depending on the normative area involved. Early toilet training is usually directed by the mother, whereas occupational training is supervised on the job by other members of the occupation or by specialists in a vocational or professional school. A great deal of socialization is deliberate, but it also occurs inadvertently when the individual picks up cues about social norms without special instruction about them.

Some part in the complex process of socialization is taken by the mass media. Either deliberately or inadvertently, the individual at various times in life probably learns some social norms from the media. It is important to remember, however, that mass communication is only one of many sources of socialization for the child and the adult. Just what specific part the mass media play is still unknown.

What kinds of data do we need in order to map out the role of mass media in socialization? First, we need data on the communications behavior of people of various age levels. Much evidence is already available on this subject. We know, for example, that even very young children spend a great deal of time with the mass media, either alone or in the company of their family or friends. But more detailed information is desirable; longitudinal studies of changes in media habits with age would be especially useful. Some evidence on changes in children's television exposure with age is available from studies contained in the surgeon general's report. Data on changes in media behavior with aging among adults have been analyzed recently by the present author.[18]

Second, more evidence is needed on the use of the media (advertently or inadvertently) as sources of social norms. Several studies suggest that people consciously refer to the media as normative sources. For instance, some women believe that they can get prescriptions for living and solving personal problems from daytime radio serials.[19] As another example, Brenda Dervin and Bradley Greenberg reported that low-income blacks are more likely than middle-class white adults to agree that people watch television because they can learn from the mistakes of others, that television shows how other people solve the same problems that they have, and that they can learn a good deal from television.[20] And Walter Gerson, in a comparison between black and white adolescents in 1966, reports that the former were more likely than white youths to use the mass media for reinforcement and acquisition of social norms about dating behavior.[21] Such findings suggest that greater consideration be given to the potentially differential role of the mass media as agents of socialization for various segments of society.

Third, we need more information on the extent to which people absorb social norms from the mass media—consciously and unconsciously, directly and, indirectly, from others who have acquired norms from the media. Here data are needed, for example, on audience identification with characters who serve as role models or reference figures for values and behavior.

Fourth, we need to know more about the relative rank of the

[18] Charles R. Wright, "Social Structure and Mass Communications Behavior: New Directions for Audience Research," in *The Idea of Social Structure: Papers in Honor of Robert K. Merton*, ed. Lewis Coser (New York: Harcourt Brace Jovanovich, 1975). For changes in children's media use, see Jack Lyle, "Television in Daily Life," in Vol. IV of the surgeon general's report cited in note 6 above.

[19] H. Herzog, "What Do We Really Know About Daytime Serial Listeners," in *Radio Research 1942–1943*, ed. Paul Lazarsfeld and Frank Stanton (New York: Duell, Sloan and Pearce, 1944), pp. 3–33.

[20] Brenda Dervin and Bradley Greenberg, "The Communication Environment of the Urban Poor," in *Current Perspectives in Mass Communication Research*, Vol. I, ed. F. Gerald Kline and Phillip J. Tichenor (Beverly Hills, Calif.: Sage Publications, 1972), Ch. 7.

[21] Walter Gerson, "Mass Media Socialization Behavior: Negro-White Differences," *Social Forces*, 45 (1966): 40–50.

mass media as normative sources among such other major agents of socialization as the family, school, and peer group. Neil Hollander, for example, has reported that a sample of one group of high school seniors cited the mass media, and especially television, as relatively more important than such traditional socializing agencies as the church, families, friends, and school in determining their ideology about war.[22] As another example, Steven Chaffee, L. Scott Ward, and Leonard Tipton reported that samples of high school juniors and seniors in Wisconsin rated the mass media as the most important sources of information and of their personal opinions about current affairs, in comparison with such alternative sources as parents, friends, and teachers.[23] These studies clearly only open the door to a problem that requires much further research.

Finally, we need to expand our investigations to include content of socialization other than explicit norms. More particularly, as has been suggested recently by Herbert Hyman, we need to examine the role of the mass media in socializing individuals to moral and social sentiments—for example, feelings of sympathy and pity toward victims of violence, war, accidents, catastrophes, and social injustice.[24]

Direct studies of media and socialization are rare, however.[25] The two studies summarized below, although not recent, illustrate very well modes of research touching upon some of the problems of socialization already mentioned. One is an investigation of children's identification with the characters in radio

[22] Neil Hollander, "Adolescents and the War: the Sources of Socialization," *Journalism Quarterly* 58 (1971): 472–479.

[23] Steven Chaffee, L. Scott Ward, and Leonard Tipton, "Mass Communication and Political Socialization," *Journalism Quarterly* 57 (1970): 647–659, 666.

[24] Herbert Hyman, "Mass Communication and Socialization," *Public Opinion Quarterly* 37 4 (Winter 1973–1974): pp. 524–540.

[25] We exclude from consideration here studies of mass media for instruction in scholastic matters, such as literacy and adult education, whether broadcast or confined to classrooms. These are important but beyond the scope of this book. Our concern here is with socialization to values, norms, and other components of culture usually considered under the sociological and social-psychological rubric of socialization. For a summary of the experiences of the Children's Television Workshop with "Sesame Street" and similar programs aimed at instruction of young children by means of television, see Gerald Lesser, *Children and Television: Lessons from Sesame Street* (New York: Random House, 1974).

space serials; the other is a study of the impact of a radio program intended to help socialize adolescents.[26]

In the first study, by Robert Zajonc, a radio program about the adventures of a space rocket was played in different versions for two groups of children between ten and fourteen years of age. The program had two leading characters, Rocky and Buddy. Rocky, a power-oriented character, tried to solve problems through his authority and direct control over others. Buddy, an affiliation-oriented leader, tried to handle problems by establishing affective associations with other people—being liked by them, being friendly or nice. One group of children heard a version of the program ("Space Masters") in which the bulk of the perils the rocket ship faced were solved by Rocky and his power-oriented approach to interpersonal relations. The other group heard stories ("Space Mission") in which Buddy, with his affiliative orientation, was more successful.

After the show the children were asked whether they would rather be like Buddy or like Rocky. Presumably, the answers would indicate whether the listeners identified with a character on the basis of the kind of person he seemed to be (tough versus friendly) or on the basis of how successful he was, regardless of his methods. With only a few exceptions the listeners chose the character who was successful. That is, listeners to "Space Masters" wanted to be like Rocky; those who heard "Space Mission" wanted to be like Buddy. Furthermore, in response to a question about why they would rather be like one character than the other, most children answered in terms of the personal attributes of the successful figure. Those who heard the version in which Buddy was successful found his affiliative attributes most attractive; listeners to the version that portrayed Rocky's success found power attributes desirable, although with some exceptions. Finally, the researchers considered whether the children had made the values represented by the heroes part of their own code, asking the children which goal would be more important for them if they were the captain of a space ship:

---

[26] Robert Zajonc, "Some Effects of Space Serials," *Public Opinion Quarterly* 18 (Winter 1954–1955): 367–374. Raymond Forer, "The Impact of a Radio Program on Adolescents," *Public Opinion Quarterly* 19 (Summer 1955): 184–194.

making sure that everybody gets along together or making sure that everybody obeys orders. Children exposed to the affiliative-oriented programs chose the first goal, whereas those who heard the power-oriented version were more likely to choose the second.

This study should be regarded as exploratory rather than as definitive. The children studied may not be representative of all children in their age group. And, as the author indicates, the effects measured may have been short-lived ones rather than basic changes in the value systems of the children. But even the demonstration of short-term effects on expressed values is of importance.

Another study, by Raymond Forer, of the impact of a radio program called "Mind Your Manners," is of special interest to the topic of socialization for two reasons. First, the program chosen made a deliberate effort to socialize its adolescent audience. Advice was given by a panel of "typical" teen-agers, who discussed personal problems submitted by the listeners. Second, the study inquired as to whether the audience followed the norms prescribed by the panel and what would happen if these norms conflicted with those prescribed by family, friends, or other agents of socialization.

Forer distributed questionnaires to a sample consisting of 2,700 Connecticut students of high school age. Students who had a knowledge of the program (a majority of the sample) were asked a series of additional questions designed to measure its impact. Most of these students thought that the advice given on the program was usually very good; seven of ten said they would ordinarily follow the advice.

What would happen if the program's advice differed from that given by others? Listeners were asked if they would follow the advice given by the program instead of that given, for example, by their father or their mother. The alternatives covered ten primary-group relations and three mass media. Of all the primary groups, by far the most powerful agent of socialization in competition with the radio program was the immediate family. About nine of ten adolescents would take the advice of their mother or sibling(s) instead of that of the program, and nearly as many would follow their father's advice. Religious leaders were ranked fairly high, with over eight of ten students giving their advice priority. The advice of an older friend, grand-parent(s), aunt, or uncle would be taken first in two of three cases. Advice from such institutional figures as teachers and recreation leaders would be followed instead of the program's in only four of ten cases. But a fairly large proportion of re-spondents (nearly 50 percent) would adhere to the program's advice in preference to that of their teen-age friends—an anoma-lous finding in view of current notions that the face-to-face adolescent peer group is one of the most important influences on youth. Finally, the program's advice would be preferred to that offered by such other mass media as books, teen-age maga-zines, and newspaper columns. This study reminds us, then, that the impact of the mass media must be evaluated in relation to the total complex of social relationships within which the audience members function before, during, and after their ex-posure to the medium.

Before closing this discussion of media and socialization, it is important to emphasize again the need for data on the func-tions and dysfunctions of *mass* communication as an instrument of socialization. We need to know, for instance, what difference it makes if social norms are acquired through the impersonal mass-distributed communications rather than through such pri-mary sources as the family, friendship, or work group. We need data on the extent to which socialization by mass communica-tions standardizes culture throughout all social levels and geo-graphical regions of the society. The role of mass communica-tions in the creation and perpetuation of a youth subculture should be explored. And we need to know the extent to which mass socialization changes the quality of the normative content transmitted, as well as whether it strengthens or weakens social control in the mass society. Research on these and similar questions will enhance our sociological perspective and under-standing of the role of mass communications in the overall process of character formation, as well as in such a specific area as juvenile delinquency.

SUCCESSFUL CAMPAIGNS AND MASS PERSUASION IN A DEMOCRACY

Throughout the twentieth century many citizens of the Western world, and especially those in democratic nations, have become increasingly concerned about the political and social power of mass communication. This concern, in its most general form, expresses itself in such broadly phrased questions as: Do the mass media really have any effect on public opinion? on elections? on attitudes toward such basic democratic values as freedom and equality? Underneath these questions may be a fear that the individual and the public can be manipulated by those who have access to the mass media. Stated slightly differently, the issue becomes: Are our opinions, attitudes, knowledge, and behavior so vulnerable that they can be changed by what we see on television, read in the newspapers, hear on the radio, and so on?

Thus phrased, the question is easily answered, but the answer is seductively simple. Of course the media affect the public. We know this from common observation and from a wealth of systematic research evidence. After all, one's perception of the world around serves to guide many of one's opinions and much of the picture of the world comes through mass communications. But the danger of this simple answer is that it may forestall our recognition of the equally important fact that not all mass communications are successful in affecting opinions, attitudes, knowledge, or behavior. The process of mass influence is far from automatic, and the public's role in this process far from passive. Consider as examples the following two early public-spirited campaigns. Although both predate the television age, they nonetheless provide instructive lessons about mass persuasion since both were the subjects of relatively rare scientific analysis.

Case 1 □ A War Bond Marathon

During World War II, Kate Smith, broadcasting over CBS radio network in an eighteen-hour marathon, during which she repeated appeals every few minutes, obtained pledges from the audience for approximately $39 million worth of United States government bonds. In a similar marathon a year later she sold $110 million worth of bonds.[27] Both events were remarkable demonstrations of the potential power for mass persuasion

---

[27] See Robert K. Merton, Marjorie Fiske, and Alberta Curtis, *Mass Persuasion: The Social Psychology of a War Bond Drive* (New York: Harper and Brothers, 1946).

available to one individual using only one major avenue for mass communication.

Case 2 □ A Public Information Campaign

In 1947 several public organizations, including the American Association for the United Nations, began an intensive six-month mass communications campaign in Cincinnati, Ohio, presenting information about the UN and world affairs. The Cincinnati Plan was to provide a social demonstration of how a large community could become informed on world issues through a mass educational campaign. Many communications facilities of Cincinnati were used extensively throughout the six months; features were run in newspapers and over the radio, special pamphlets, signs, and posters were distributed; meetings and speeches were arranged.

What was the net result of the campaign? Apparently little change was achieved among the public. At the request of the campaign's sponsors an evaluation of its impact was made by the National Opinion Research Center (NORC) of the University of Chicago. Using the data gathered from a random sample of Cincinnatians before and after the campaign, the researchers detected no significant influence on the public's knowledge, interest, opinions, or behavior concerning the UN or world affairs. For instance, before the campaign fully 30 percent of the adults in Cincinnati could not say what the main purpose of the UN was and did not even indicate familiarity with its general concern with keeping the peace. After the campaign 28 percent of the Cincinnatians, judged by the same criteria, still were unacquainted with the UN—an educational gain of only 2 percent of the public.[28]

With respect to serious communications campaigns, the Smith broadcast illustrates success, and the Cincinnati Plan illustrates failure. But both cases point to the conclusion that the critical

---

[28] For a fuller account of the campaign and its evaluation, see Shirley Star and Helen Hughes, "Report on an Educational Campaign: The Cincinnati Plan for the United Nations," *American Journal of Sociology* 55 (January 1950): 389–400; and National Opinion Research Center, *Cincinnati Looks at the United Nations* and *Cincinnati Looks Again* Reports No. 37 and 37A (mimeographed).

consideration here is not whether or not mass media campaigns have any effect on the public, but under what *conditions* they do so. What are some of the factors, especially social and psychological, that help determine their success or failure?

For purposes of analysis it is convenient to view the communication process in several stages, starting with the formulation and transmission of a message, through the stages of audience exposure and immediate response or reaction to the message, and culminating in some short- or long-term effects. A breakdown in effectiveness at any stage during the process may cause the ultimate failure of a mass communications campaign. Our discussion will focus on the social and psychological factors affecting audience exposure, reactions, and effects.[29]

Audience coverage is an obvious precondition for effective communication. A variety of other factors also determine the effect of the message, but it cannot be influential at all if it does not reach its target. For instance, adequate physical output must be maintained in a form accessible to the public. But there are other than physical requirements that must be met if a communication is to be effective. For clues to such requirements let us consider the Cincinnati campaign again. What went wrong?

In analyzing the dynamics of the Cincinnati campaign the researchers from NORC asked: How may people were exposed to the campaign during the six months? What kinds of people were reached? Who was missed? What effect did the campaign have on those people it reached? Just where in the total process of mass education did the campaign fail? Through the answers to such questions the major cause of failure could be pinpointed by the researchers. They found that the campaign had reached only individuals who were already predisposed to pay attention to it because of their initial interest in world affairs and the UN or because of their favorable attitude toward the UN. Bear in mind that there was no dearth of communication output during the campaign, nor was the material inaccessible to the public. The campaign failed because it did not reach those most in need of its message from the point of view of the sponsors.

---

[29] For an earlier but fuller discussion see Charles R. Wright, "Evaluating Mass Media Campaigns," *International Social Science Bulletin* 7 (1955): 417–430.

That is, it did not reach the ill-informed, apathetic, or hostile people in the city.

Was the behavior of Cincinnatians in this instance idiosyncratic—specific perhaps to the theme of support for the United Nations? No. As noted in Chapter 4, similar behavior has been observed in other studies of serious educational and propaganda campaigns in a variety of areas, for example, public health programs and Presidential election campaigns. The Cincinnatians' behavior is an example of *selective exposure*—a common and major obstacle to successful communication campaigns.[30]

Even if individuals happen to be exposed to communications contrary to their interests and predispositions, the potential impact of the message may be weakened, even distorted, through *selective perception* and *selective interpretation* of the content. A rare opportunity for studying these phenomena in a natural setting was provided in 1960, when the two major candidates for the Presidency of the United States engaged in a series of televised debates. It is estimated that the first debate between John F. Kennedy and Richard M. Nixon was seen by approximately 70 million adults and by 10 to 15 million younger people in the United States and that approximately 80 percent of the population of the United States saw at least one of the four debates. More than thirty studies were made of the public response to the debates; the major results have been compiled and analyzed in *The Great Debates*.[31]

Studies indicate that Democrats and Republicans were about equally likely to view the debates; presumably, the appearance of both candidates overcame the barrier of selective exposure to communications only from the party of one's choice. By and large, however, viewers tended to perceive the candidate of their choice as having won the debates. This is not to say that the debates had no effect; in particular there appears to be support

---

[30] We refer here to de facto selective exposure, a regularity in patterns of exposure to mass communications that may or may not be caused by individual motives. See note 34, Chapter 4. See also David Sears and Jonathan Freedman, "Selective Exposure to Information: A Critical Review," *Public Opinion Quarterly* 31 (1967): 194–213.

[31] Sidney Kraus, ed., *The Great Debates* (Bloomington: Indiana University Press, 1962). See especially Ch. 11, Elihu Katz and Jacob Feldman, "The Debates in Light of Research: A Survey of Surveys."

for the conclusion that at least the first debate strengthened Democratic support for their own candidate, Kennedy. But there was little or no evidence that voters were converted from their original predispositions and switched to the opposite political party. Selective perception and interpretation strengthened the viewers' commitment to their own party's candidate.

Dramatic evidence of selective perception and interpretation is also provided in a study by Patricia Kendall and Katherine Wolfe, concerning reactions to a series of antiprejudice cartoons.[32] The cartoons satirized a highly prejudiced character, Mr. Biggott, who was depicted expressing hostility toward American minority groups in a variety of situations. The pictures were shown to 160 men. Detailed interviews, lasting from one to three hours, were held with each man to determine his understanding and reaction to the cartoons.

The interviews revealed that the antiprejudice message was *misunderstood* by approximately two-thirds of the sample. Furthermore, many of the men not only misunderstood the message but actually reversed its meaning, believing that the cartoons were designed to create racial disturbances and to intensify existing prejudices. The explanation of these misunderstandings is complicated. However, one finding is especially relevant for the discussion of selective interpretation. It turns out that the major correlate of understanding or misunderstanding was not a man's formal skills (as inferred from the amount of formal schooling he had had, for example), but rather the presence or absence of certain predispositions to understand. Among the most important of these were the man's original prejudices and his awareness of the problem of prejudice in the world. To illustrate, among men who were themselves prejudiced and not concerned with prejudice as a social problem, three of four were likely to misunderstand the cartoons.

A recent example of research bearing on both selective exposure and selective perception is provided by Neil Vidmar and Milton Rokeach's study of viewers of the popular television

---

[32] Patricia Kendall and Katherine Wolf, "The Analysis of Deviant Cases in Communications Research," in *Communications Research 1948–1949*, ed. Paul Lazarsfeld and Frank Stanton, pp. 152–179. See also Eunice Cooper and Marie Jahoda, "The Evasion of Propaganda," *Journal of Psychology* 23 (1947): 15–25.

comedy program "All in the Family."[33] The central character in this show is Archie Bunker, who is portrayed as a bigot. Bunker's "humor" frequently consists of racial, ethnic, and sexist slurs. The situation comedy is presented as a form of satire on racial prejudice and bigotry, openly violating previous television norms against expressions of racial and ethnic slurs. Defenders of the program have praised it as a form of successful entertainment that can have the beneficial social effect of reducing prejudice by poking fun at bigotry and by making viewers aware of their own undesirable prejudices. Critics have charged that the show may actually be encouraging racism and prejudice and may be especially harmful to impressionable children.

Vidmar and Rokeach recast the issue in terms of the possibility that prejudiced and unprejudiced persons differ in their exposure to the show and, when they do view it, differ in their interpretations of it in line with their predispositions. To test such possibilities, the researchers studied a sample of adolescents in Illinois and adults in Ontario, Canada. Respondents were classified as relatively high or low in prejudice on the basis of questionnaire responses, and then comparisons were made of their reactions to the program. Frequent viewers of the program among the American adolescents (but not among the Canadian adults) were more likely than infrequent viewers to be relatively high in prejudice, to admire the bigoted Archie more than his "liberal" son-in-law, Mike, and to condone Archie's ethnic slurs. The researchers conclude that highly prejudiced adolescents are more prone than less prejudiced ones to watch the show, a demonstration of selective exposure. Some patterns of response among these modern television viewers are strikingly similar to those found in the study of Mr. Biggott cartoons, a quarter century earlier. Vidmar and Rokeach found that highly prejudiced persons were more likely than less prejudiced individuals to admire Archie, to perceive him as making more sense (although relatively few viewers actually said this), and to see him as winning at the end of the program. The authors interpret such

---

[33] Neil Vidmar and Milton Rokeach, "Archie Bunker's Bigotry: A Study in Selective Perception and Exposure," *Journal of Communication* 24 (Winter 1974): 36–47.

differences as supporting the hypothesis of selective perception. The study is limited, of course, by the size and other restrictions of the samples used, as well as by other methodological considerations. Therefore, as the authors note, it would be desirable to have replications with more extensive and representative samples. The study nonetheless serves as a timely reminder of the continuing interest in selective exposure and selective perception as factors affecting the possible reception of a program's "intended message."

But selective exposure and selective perception are not the only barriers to communication. Two experts in public opinion research, Herbert Hyman and Paul Sheatsley, have codified some of the major reasons why information campaigns fail.[34] Hyman and Sheatsley identify five psychological characteristics of human beings that affect their exposure to campaigns and their absorption of the message. First, repeated social surveys have revealed the existence of a hard core of chronic "know nothings" —people who know nothing about most topics with which a campaign might deal and whose social and psychological make-up makes them especially hard to reach, no matter what the level or nature of information contained in the campaign. Second, there are members of large groups in the population who admit that they have little or no interest in the public issues around which campaigns are usually organized—an effective barrier, since interest is a strong determinant both of exposure to and absorption of information. Third, people tend to expose themselves to material that is congenial with their prior attitudes and to avoid exposure to that which is not congenial (one possible cause of de facto selective exposure). Fourth, as noted, there is selective perception and interpretation of content following exposure. People perceive, absorb, interpret, and remember content differently, according to such mediating factors as their wishes, motives and prior attitudes. Finally, changes in views or behavior following exposure to a message may be differentially affected by the individual's initial predispositions and attitudes.

Through laboratory and field experiments and through practi-

---

[34] Herbert Hyman and Paul Sheatsley, "Some Reasons Why Information Campaigns Fail," *Public Opinion Quarterly* 11 (Fall 1947): 412–423.

cal experience in propaganda and education, quite a bit has been learned about other factors that affect response to communications.[35] Interpretation of these findings requires considerable caution, however. We never can be certain that the findings obtained under controlled conditions of an experiment or wartime field conditions would also appear under other circumstances.

Excellent social psychological experiments have been made in this area, among them the studies conducted by the late Carl Hovland and his colleagues.[36] Their research has shown, for example, that the audience's reactions to a message are affected by its image of the communicator—the communicator's social responsibility and intentions, trustworthiness, and orientation to education or propaganda. Thus, people tend initially to resist messages coming from sources they regard with suspicion; but later some individuals change their opinions in the direction advocated by the communicator.[37] This phenomenon of delayed conversion (which was also observed in experiments with army training films during World War II) has been labeled the "sleeper effect." One explanation of it is that the message was initially unsuccessful because of suspicion toward the communicator rather than because of any deficiencies in the arguments used. Some time later, there is a dissociation of content and source in the audience's mind. The information and arguments that had

---

[35] For examples, see Walter Weiss, "Effects of the Mass Media of Communication," in *Handbook of Social Psychology*, 2d ed., Gardner Lindzey and Elliot Aronson (Reading, Mass.: Addison-Wesley, 1969), Vol. 5, pp. 77–195. See also William McGuire, "Persuasion, Resistance, and Attitude Change," in Ithiel de Sola Pool et al., eds., *Handbook of Communication* (Chicago: Rand McNally, 1973), Ch. 9.

[36] For examples, see Carl Hovland, Arthur Lumsdaine, and Fred Sheffield, *Experiments on Mass Communication* (Princeton, N.J.: Princeton University Press, 1949); Carl Hovland, Irving Janis, and Harold Kelley, *Communication and Persuasion* (New Haven, Conn.: Yale University Press, 1953); Carl Hovland et al., *The Order of Presentation in Persuasion* (New Haven, Conn.: Yale University Press, 1957); Irving Janis et al., *Personality and Persuasibility* (New Haven, Conn.: Yale University Press, 1959); Milton Rosenberg et al., *Attitude Organization and Change* (New Haven, Conn.: Yale University Press, 1960); Muzafir Sherif and Carl Hovland, *Social Judgment* (New Haven, Conn.: Yale University Press, 1961).

[37] Carl Hovland and Walter Weiss, "Source Credibility and Communication Effectiveness," *Public Opinion Quarterly* 15 (Winter 1951–1952): 635–650.

been heard, now no longer tainted by memory of the original untrustworthy source, were able to change opinions. Subsequent experiments lend support to this hypothesis.

Hovland's research group, and others, also have experimented with how effectiveness of communications is influenced by variations in the nature of the content and the audience situation. Experiments have been made with fear-rousing appeals, one-sided arguments, audience participation, and other procedures. The results underscore the importance of research on the long-term consequences of mass communications as well as on their immediate effects.

With so many social and psychological barriers to success, one may wonder how effective mass persuasion is ever achieved. Yet, under favorable conditions, the mass media can give a communicator great power. An illustration is the war bond drive mentioned earlier in the chapter.

An excellent analysis of the social and psychological factors in the success of Kate Smith's marathon is presented in *Mass Persuasion* by Robert Merton, Marjorie Fiske, and Alberta Curtis.[38] Merton and his colleagues combined a content analysis of the themes in the broadcast with focused interviews with a sample of the program's listeners, some of whom had pledged to buy bonds. These detailed interviews were supplemented with a survey of approximately 1,000 New Yorkers, which tested some of the hypotheses and observations from the smaller sample.

The researchers found the broadcast effective, among other reasons, because of a combination of characteristics of the event itself, the public image of its star, the themes employed, and the predispositions of the audience.

First, the campaign itself was defined, both by the broadcaster and by the listeners, as a unique event. Against a background of commercial radio programs and other common forms of advertising, the marathon stood out as something extraordinary. It caught the attention of the audience. Furthermore, by its very nature a marathon gave the communicator a variety of advantages, for example, by increasing the audience's motivation to continue listening in order to hear the outcome and by permitting

---

[38] Merton et al., *Mass Persuasion*.

arguments to cumulate and to be repeated in several forms.[39]

Not only was the broadcast perceived as different from ordinary commercial events but Kate Smith herself was regarded as especially suitable for the role of seller of War Bonds. The New York survey indicated that technical competence in financial matters was not the main quality people believed the role called for, but such personal qualities as sincerity, patriotism, and benevolence. Kate Smith was, to many, a person especially endowed as a moral leader, rather than only an entertainer or a businesswoman. Furthermore, the very act of conducting the marathon validated her sincerity, as Merton put it, by the "propaganda-of-the-deed."

The themes in the broadcast were especially suitable to the patriotic, sincere character symbolized by its star. At no time during the marathon was there any emphasis on the "profane" aspects of bonds—their value as financial investments or their role in curbing inflation. Rather, the program stressed the more sacred themes. Especially prominent was the motif of sacrifice—by servicemen, by other civilians, and by the broadcaster herself. Other themes concerned participation in a common enterprise, competition between communities, familial values, the ease with which a pledge could be made (simply pick up the telephone), and Kate Smith's personal desire to make the campaign a success.

Content analysis could identify the variety of themes used,

---

[39] Marathon broadcasting continues to be employed as a form of political persuasion and of fund raising in the television age, sometimes with apparent success, at other times without. As an example, former Senator William Knowland conducted a twenty-hour telethon during his race for the governorship of California in 1958. Wilbur Schramm and Richard Carter studied the effectiveness of this political telethon on the basis of interviews with more than 500 respondents in San Francisco. They concluded that the telethon did not lead to any large-scale changes in viewers' intentions to vote, nor to any major cognitive and attitudinal changes, although it did appear to confirm the impressions that viewers had of the senator and reinforced their initial voting intentions. (Wilbur Schramm and Richard Carter, "Effectiveness of a Political Telethon," *Public Opinion Quarterly* 23 (Spring 1959): 121–127.) Although not documented by social research, a telethon held by the Democratic party in July 1974 appears to have been successful in fund raising. The Democratic National Committee stated that it netted nearly $4.5 million from its third annual fund-raising telethon out of a total of $7.1 million in pledges received during a weekend of telecasting. (Christopher Lydon, "Democrats Hail TV Fund-Raising," *New York Times*, July 2, 1974, p. 23.)

but focused interviews with the audience were necessary in order to evaluate the themes' effectiveness. Not every theme had equal impact upon all members of the audience. Predispositions toward war bonds in general and the Third War Loan drive in particular seemed to make the audience members differentially responsive to one or another of the themes. The orientation of some listeners toward war bonds was fairly sentimental and emotional; others were less involved. Some people had already planned to buy a bond during the Third War Loan drive; others had not. Those who had both emotional involvement and intent to buy may be considered the favorably predisposed members of the audience. They had only to be persuaded to buy the bond at that moment and from Kate Smith. For this group the facilitation theme (just pick up the telephone) seemed to have great impact, presumably because it saved them the effort of going out to buy their bonds. Other themes appealed to persons with different predispositions.

Especially interesting is the process by which the group called the "susceptibles" were persuaded. These people had an emotional involvement in war bonds but had no intention of buying one from the drive. Their reluctance reflected in part their feeling that they were already doing their share through systematic purchases of bonds, perhaps through a payroll savings plan. (There appears to have developed at the time an informal social norm that patriotic citizens were doing their share if they invested about 10 percent of their income in bonds.) In convincing these people that their past behavior was inadequate, the themes of sacrifice apparently were most successful. By stressing the greater sacrifices being made by servicemen and other civilians, Kate Smith was able to overcome the audience's complacency, lower their self-esteem, and arouse some guilt feelings. The susceptibles came to the conclusion that they were not doing as much as other good citizens to help win the war. Kate Smith's own right to point up this deficiency and to call for greater effort from her audience was established by her favorable public image combined with the sacrifice she herself was making by conducting the marathon. Since it was clear that her actions exceeded the ordinary, she was not asking her audience to do more than she was doing. Next she prescribed the new behavior that could raise the self-esteem of the audience and reduce guilt feelings: buy a *sacrifice* bond. Even the mechanism by which the deed could be performed was provided—simply use the telephone. Finally, as moral leader, she rewarded the new behavior by reporting on the progress of the campaign, citing dramatic incidents from the telephone calls received, and so on.

Other factors contributing to the success of the broadcast are detailed in *Mass Persuasion*. These include the fact that there was no counterpropaganda.

To the many social psychological factors that have been illustrated here through the work of Hyman, Hovland, Merton, and others, we must remember to add such sociological variables as have been discussed earlier. For example, the social groups to which each audience member belongs or refers will influence his or her chances of being exposed to any media campaign, the perception and interpretation of the content, and its impact. The social context sets limits also to the range of behavior that any message can produce. For example, enemy troops stationed far behind the front lines can hardly surrender, no matter how persuasive the appeals of psychological warfare might be. As another example, studies of Allied psychological warfare against the German Wehrmacht during World War II have shown that the early, politically focused propaganda had little effect in terms of surrender of troops. Two social scientists, Edward Shils and Morris Janowitz, discovered that the German soldiers were held together less by any political dogma than by a tightly knit arrangement of primary groups within the army.[40] Hence propaganda that stressed political themes had little impact. Few of the men could be persuaded to surrender, because each was integrated into a primary group whose members depended upon one another for friendship and the other human satisfactions that sustain morale. There was little social possibility for desertion, except for those few soldiers who (for one reason or another) were social isolates, who had not been accepted and integrated into the primary group. Allied propaganda became more effective later, when it abandoned the political emphasis and stressed such themes as individual survival, group survival, and the

---

[40] Edward Shils and Morris Janowitz, "Cohesion and Disintegration in the Wehrmacht in World War II," *Public Opinion Quarterly* 12 (Summer 1948): 280–315.

strategically hopeless position of some of the troops. Themes of individual survival appeared most successful among men who had become physically (hence socially) isolated from their units. Propaganda that utilized primary-group pressures—for example, leaflets that persuaded the men to begin talking to one another about their military position, their desire to stay alive for their family's sake, and the possibility of honorable surrender—were sometimes quite effective.

These cases reemphasize the importance of viewing mass communications as functioning within the larger sociological perspective of the culture, social organization, and human groups. This has been a recurrent theme in the present chapter and, indeed, in the entire book.

Some other aspects of the social effects of mass communications have been touched upon at other parts of the work: the impact of mass communications upon voting, for example, was discussed in some detail in Chapter 4, with reference to face-to-face communication and opinion leadership. Of course, a complete treatment of social effects would consider many other topics, such as the meaning of mass communication for the democratic practice of trial by jury.[41] To what extent does coverage of crimes by mass communication affect the probability of finding jurors who have not already formed an opinion about a case? Or how might radio and television coverage of a trial affect the behavior of witnesses, jury, lawyers, and other participants? Would such on-the-spot coverage jeopardize the trial system by turning each trial into a spectacle? Or would it enhance the proceedings by making the actions of the participants open to immediate surveillance by the public?

Here, as throughout the book, our purpose has been to suggest rather than to exhaust the sociologically exciting aspects of mass communication. The reader who is encouraged by this analysis to explore some topics further will find the Selected Readings a useful guide to the subject.

---

[41] For an early study see Walter Wilcox, "The Press, the Jury and the Behavioral Sciences," *Journalism Monograph*, No. 9 (October 1968). For a discussion of some possible implications of the issue of mass media coverage of trials and other issues, see Ben Bagdikian, "First Amendment Revision," *Columbia Journalism Review* 13 (May-June 1974): 39–48. See also a symposium on due process in *Journal of Communication* 24 (Summer 1974).

IMPACT OF THE NEW COMMUNICATIONS TECHNOLOGY

Major strides in mass media technology have been made during the past decade that promise to change the shape and powers of the mass media. Foremost among these are cable television (with its accompanying plan for communication back from the audience member to the communicator) and communication satellites. Joined to our ever-improving computer technology, the prospects for social impact seem awesome—but no more awesome, perhaps, than those anticipated upon the introduction of other major communication changes, such as radio broadcasting and television. A sense of history adds perspective. Forecasts about social effects are, understandably, mixed: enthusiasts look optimistically toward future social benefits of the new media; critics fix upon expected social damage.[42] Cable television is seen by some as breaking the bonds restricting telecasts to a small number of channels, opening the door to a greater variety of shows, programing to meet minority tastes, local program origination, and other benefits. Pessimists see cable television as evolving, at best, into a more expensive (to the consumer) array of programs similar to those now available through direct telecasts. They foresee it, at worst, as developing into a tightly controlled instrument for propaganda, government surveillance of citizens, and other oppressive intrusions into the private lives of individuals, not unlike those fictionalized in George Orwell's once futuristic novel, *1984*. Satellites are seen by optimists as enabling people-to-people communications across national boundaries; pessimists see them as potential vehicles for international propaganda and cultural invasion.

It is too early to forecast with confidence what the future will bring. Probably, the social effects of the new technology, like the old, will be mixed: some good, some bad, some trivial. The functional framework outlined in our opening chapter should serve to alert the readers to some of the possibilities and should protect them from an overly simplistic anticipation of totally functional or totally dysfunctional consequences.

---

[42] See as examples, Wilbur Schramm, Philip Coombs, Friedrich Kahnert, and Jack Lyle, *The New Media: Memo to Educational Planners* (UNESCO: International Institute for Educational Planning, 1967); George Gerbner, Larry Gross, and William Melody (eds.), *Communication Technology and Social Policy* (New York: John Wiley, 1973).

Equally important, the sociological framework developed throughout this book will, we hope, suggest some of the key areas that must be addressed by future research on the new technology. How will the new techniques become institutionalized and incorporated into their respective social systems? What will be the organizational framework within which the new communicators will work, and what will be the restraints? Who will have access to these techniques of mass communication? What will their audiences be like? Who will make use of the media, for what purposes? How will this use be combined with other means of communication? Which members of the new audiences will play a more active role, especially when given the opportunity to "talk back"? How will content be selected, by whom, and with what resultant product? What will be the differential social effects among various members of particular societies and around the globe?

Such questions reflect, as we hope our discussion throughout the book has done, the need for consideration of mass communications within the broader framework of social structure and cultural context. If our sociological perspective on mass communication has a theme, that is it.

Selected Readings

GENERAL WORKS ON MASS COMMUNICATION

W. Phillips Davison and Frederick T. C. Yu, eds., *Mass Communication Research: Major Issues and Future Directions*. New York: Praeger, 1974.

Melvin De Fleur. *Theories of Mass Communication*, 2nd ed. New York: McKay, 1970.

Alex S. Edelstein. *Perspectives in Mass Communication*. Copenhagen: Einar Harcks Forlag, 1966.

F. Gerald Kline and Phillip J. Tichenor, eds. *Current Perspectives in Mass Communication Research*. Sage Annual Review of Communication Research, Vol. I. Beverly Hills, Calif.: Sage Publications, 1972.

Denis McQuail. *Towards a Sociology of Mass Communications*. London: Collier-Macmillan, 1969.

Harold Mendelsohn. *Mass Entertainment*. New Haven, Conn.: College and University Press, 1966.

Ithiel de Sola Pool et al., eds. *Handbook of Communication*. Chicago: Rand McNally, 1973.

Wilbur Schramm and Donald F. Roberts, eds. *The Process and Effects of Mass Communication*, rev. ed. Urbana: University of Illinois Press, 1971.

Jeremy Tunstall, ed. *Media Sociology: A Reader*. Urbana: University of Illinois Press, 1970.

SPECIAL TOPICS

Functional Analysis

Robert K. Merton. *Social Theory and Social Structure*. Glencoe, Ill.: Free Press, 1957.

172   *Selected Readings*

Charles R. Wright, "Functional Analysis and Mass Communications Revisited," in *The Uses and Gratification Approach to Mass Communications Research,* ed. Jay Blumler and Elihu Katz. Sage Annual Review of Communication Research, Vol. III. Beverly Hills, Calif.: Sage Publications, 1975.

Communication Systems

George Gerbner, Larry Gross, and William Melody, eds. *Communications Technology and Social Policy.* New York: John Wiley, 1973.

Fred Siebert, Theodore Peterson, and Wilbur Schramm. *Four Theories of the Press.* Urbana: University of Illinois Press, 1956.

Mass Communicators

Muriel Cantor. *The Hollywood TV Producer.* New York: Basic Books, 1971.

Peter Halmos, ed. *The Sociology of Mass-Media Communicators. The Sociological Review Monograph 13*; Keele, Straffordshire: University of Keele, 1969.

Audiences

Jay Blumler and Elihu Katz, eds. *The Uses and Gratification Approach to Mass Communications Research.* Sage Annual Review of Communication Research, Vol. III. Beverly Hills, Calif.: Sage Publications, 1975.

Robert T. Bower. *Television and the Public.* New York: Holt, Rinehart & Winston, 1973.

Elihu Katz and Paul F. Lazarsfeld. *Personal Influence.* Glencoe, Ill.: Free Press, 1950.

Communication Content

George Gerbner et al., eds. *The Analysis of Communication Content: Developments in Scientific Theories and Computer Techniques.* New York: John Wiley, 1969.

Ole Holsti. *Content Analysis for the Social Sciences and Humanities.* Reading, Mass.: Addison-Wesley, 1969.

Communication Effects

Joseph Klapper. *The Effects of Mass Media.* Glencoe, Ill.: Free Press, 1960.

Kurt Lang and Gladys Engel Lang. *Politics and Television.* Chicago: Quadrangle Books, 1968.

Robert K. Merton, Marjorie Fiske, and Alberta Curtis. *Mass Persuasion: The Social Psychology of a War Bond Drive.* New York: Harper & Brothers, 1946.

Wilbur Schramm, Jack Lyle, and Edwin Parker, *Television in the Lives of Our Children.* Stanford, Calif.: Stanford University Press, 1961.

Surgeon General's Scientific Advisory Committee on Television and Social Behavior. *Television and Growing Up: The Impact of Televised Violence.* Washington, D.C.: U.S. Government Printing Office, 1972.

Research Methods

Charles Y. Glock, ed. *Survey Research in the Social Sciences.* New York: Russell Sage Foundation, 1967.

Herbert H. Hyman, *Secondary Analysis of Sample Surveys.* New York: John Wiley, 1972.

Paul F. Lazarsfeld, Ann K. Pasanella, and Morris Rosenberg, eds. *Continuities in the Language of Social Research.* New York: Free Press, 1972.

Gardner Lindzey and Elliot Aronson, eds. *The Handbook of Social Psychology,* 2nd ed. Reading, Mass.: Addison-Wesley, 1968. Vol. II, *Research Methods.*

Charles R. Wright is Professor of Communications and Sociology at the University of Pennsylvania, where he is a member of the Annenberg School of Communications and of the University's Department of Sociology. Formerly, he was with the sociology departments of the University of California, Los Angeles, and Columbia University. From 1967 to 1969 he served as Program Director in Sociology and Social Psychology at the National Science Foundation. Professor Wright's published work includes several coauthored books, among them *The Enduring Effects of Education*, as well as numerous contributions to anthologies and professional journals. The first edition of *Mass Communication* has been translated into Italian, Spanish, Portugese, and Japanese.